AGENDA

Dwelling Places

An appreciation of John Burnside

AGENDA

CONTENTS

ESSAYS

POEMS

Front and back cover and artwork throughout this issue: Johnny Marsh.
Johnny Marsh gained a BA in Fine Art from Goldsmiths College, and
an MA in Art Psychotherapy. He works as a part-time gardener and for
Mencap. He lives in Mayfield, East Sussex.

Editorial

In these difficult times, of cut-backs and financial hardships, poetry journals such as *Agenda* struggle to survive. The Arts Council's support is vital, but we have to show an increasing surge of subscribers on our list in order to have the optimum chance of maintaining Arts Council funding every year.

Therefore I address this to every subscriber, every reader and every poetry lover: **we need you. Please** do all you can to **get at least two friends to subscribe to** *Agenda*. It is very good value for money – soul food! – and ensures that you are at the cutting edge of a poetry that matters, that is life-giving, consolatory, uplifting, penetrative, capable of praise and understanding; that has a musical force of its own which should not be lived without. **Two extra subscription forms** (as well as the tear-off subscription form at the back of this issue) are being inserted into each copy of this issue to facilitate you in getting two friends on board as subscribers. We will so appreciate you doing your best.

And, of course, please make sure you do not forget to renew your subscriptions promptly.

In these days of online poetry magazines, kindle books – journals on paper such as *Agenda*, whose pages swish as they turn, whose spines hold them together, whose margins can be scribbled upon, whose print can be yellowed by the sun or crinkled by rainwater, need YOU, their reader and appreciator to preserve them and to ensure their continuance as carefully on your book shelves or window sills as in your hearts.

Siân Thomas (who has two poems in this issue) is coming on to the *Agenda* 'team' as an editorial assistant. You may well receive emails from her.

Many thanks for all your support, and help.

Patricia McCarthy
Marcus Frederick

AGENDA
Poetry Competition

Closing Date May 31st 2011   Details on www.agendapoetry.co.uk

RESULTS TO BE ANNOUNCED, IN NEXT ISSUE OF *AGENDA*

Introduction

This special double issue of *Agenda*, 'Dwelling Places', focusing on an important poet of our time, or indeed of any time, John Burnside, does, I hope, speak for itself. Burnside's impressive body of poetry, as I commented at the start of my interview with him, seems to breathe out and in, with a natural flow all of its own.

I first heard John Burnside reading in a darkly lit room in Brighton many years ago before he was known at all. I was so impressed by his poetry that I got William Cookson, the founding editor of *Agenda*, to take especial note of his poetry – which he did, and indeed valued it highly. Hence this issue has been long in brewing and is gathered now with a mighty good head on it for all to imbibe.

The essays, by both well-known academics and poets, and also by young poets and critics all illuminate Burnside's poetry, showing it in variegated lights and perspectives, highlighting its lyrical and narrative power, its technical virtuosity and thematic progression.

Important to note: in *Agenda*'s **special website supplement**, (www. agendapoetry.co.uk), there are further enlightening and original essays on John Burnside by **John Kinsella, Alan Stubbs, Maitreyabandhu** and **Jaime Robles**, including **a new translation piece by John Burnside**. The pieces by Kinsella and Burnside will be pasted up as soon as they are ready, hot off the press, so it is well worth visiting the site frequently. Maitreyabandhu posits, from a Buddhist point of view, that our capacity to sense directly the life around us is fundamental to any genuine spiritual life. He shows Burnside, with his 'meditative, estranged, yet intimate music', feeling alive in a world that is alive in the same way as he is, yet suffers from man's general 'atrophy of kinship' with it. Jaime Robles offers a detailed and inspiring analysis of the imagery in Burnside's 'Annunciations', showing the influence on him of Renaissance paintings. Her essay branches out to include excerpts from Burnside's novels alongside the poetry. Alan Stubbs' essay, 'Reading Burnside', offers a fresh, invigorating look at approaching the bard. Readers will agree that Burnside's poems 'connect up patterns of thought, and map them out into landscapes that feel as if they are as familiar to us, and removed from us, as those places that we knew well as children', finding for us 'the newly discovered strangenesses of ordinary things' and 'a heightened reality'.

Stubbs' essay gave me the odd little coincidental connection with Burnside that I have. He points out how Burnside, as a child, had his 'first brush with metaphor' when looking at a green and gold tin of golden syrup, with a lion on it and bees flying up from its flesh. I, too, as a child, was transfixed by this image as, for quite some time, all I would eat was Tate & Lyle's golden syrup – on cornflakes, bread, on everything. Since I was repelled by meat, my father tried to put me off the syrup by telling me that all honey-bees came out of the lion's flesh!

The poets here, from England, Ireland, Scotland and Wales, whose voices ring out specially and individually, all donate, too, their different kinds of honourings to Burnside.

Very many thanks to everyone involved.

Patricia McCarthy

Two special new collections from AGENDA Editions

James Simpson - *The Untenanted Room* (£10)

Woodcuts by Carolyn Trant

The Untenanted Room, with its elusive and haunting power, is unlike anything else I know of since Eliot and Hughes. It holds together a mythic personal narrative with the desolate gravity of our present general condition, in vigorous contemporary language which draws strength from its ancient roots and its kinship with the natural world, which we despoil even as it sustains us.

Lindsay Clarke

It is an impressive work, deeply serious, ambitious, and powerful. It addresses important issues; indeed, the 'place' where we are: 'that place/not properly inhabited,/swept clean, adrift, cut off,/hung on the grid of numbers'. Its language has a strong Anglo-Saxon feel, which corresponds to a feeling for earth, landscape, and the relation between language and the organic and animal creation.

Jeremy Hooker

Andrew McNeillie – Losers Keepers (£9)

> By day the draft under the door
> and a deep window's long skies
> turned his head from print to thought
> and what precedes them both.

'No halfers . . .' one version has it, 'losers weepers, finders keepers.' But Andrew McNeillie in these poems has halved things to make a paradox. 'Finders keepers' reminds him too much of the rough justice of schoolboys and emperors. 'Losers weepers' on the other hand he considers altogether too melancholy. 'Losers keepers' offers a way through, and as Robert Frost said, 'The best way out is always through.'

We live in and through our losses day by day. At the time they may seem like gains. But they are all fleeting. We keep a hold on what we can of them. This is the work attempted by these poems, chiefly in two territories, in Ireland and Scotland, with a triangulation to 'the ancient shades, the ghosts of youth' in Oxford. Somewhat in the spirit of latter-day lyrical ballads, they include elegies or memorials to both obscure lives and more prominent ones, and lyrics that speak from the extremities of living memory.

Both the above books can be ordered from: Agenda, The Wheelwrights, Fletching Street, Mayfield, East Sussex TN20 6TL or telephone 01435 873703. Visa and MasterCard accepted. Cheques payable to *Agenda*.

OUT OF THE EATER
AND OUT OF THE STRONG
(JUDGES·14·14)
CAME FORTH MEAT
CAME FORTH SWEETNESS.

ONCE UPON A TIME ARISTAEUS WAS GRANTED THE GIFT OF TALKING TO THE BEES. HE HAD BEEN WANDERING OUT OF GRIEF FOR THE DEATH OF HIS SON ACTEON, TORN APART BY HIS OWN HOUNDS. BEWARE OF GODDESSES BATHING, BE DISCREET DIANA IS A HUNTRESS BY NATURE. ARISTAEUS GAINED SOME SOLACE FROM THE BEES. ONE DAY THEY SICKENED AND DIED, DISTRAUGHT HE SOUGHT OUT HIS MOTHER, THE NYMPH CYRENE. SHE SENT HIM TO PROTEUS, THE OLD MAN OF THE SEA HE WOULD KNOW WHAT TO DO. CATCH HIM AS HE SLEEPS AMONGST HIS SEALS AND HOLD HIM TIGHT REGARDLESS OF HIS SHAPE-SHIFTING. THIS HE DID, HOLDING ON FOR DEAR LIFE AS HE CHANGED FROM SEAL, TO SNAKE, TO LION, TO WOLF AND ALL MANNER OF FEROCIOUS BEASTS, TO WATER, TO EARTH, TO AIR, TO FIRE, BUT STILL HE KEPT HIS GRIP. PROTEUS, EXHAUSTED RETURNED TO HIS ORIGINAL FORM AND DIVULGED THAT THE DEATH OF THE BEES AND HIS ILL FORTUNE WAS DUE TO THE DEATH OF EURYDICE, WHOSE DEMISE ARISTAEUS HAD ACCIDENTALLY CAUSED, SHE HAD BEEN BITTEN BY A POISONOUS SERPENT WHILE FLEEING FROM ARISTAEUS'S. AMOROUS PURSUIT. CYRENE HAD BEEN WATCHING, AND AFTER HER SON HAD POLITELY THANKED PROTEUS SHE WENT TO HIM AND TOLD HIM HOW TO APPEASE THE ANGER OF THE NYMPHS AND ATONE FOR EURYDICES DEATH. FIRST SACRIFICE FOUR BULLS AND FOUR HEIFERS, THE FINEST BEASTS. THESE HE SHOULD LEAVE IN A SHELTER, OPEN ON EACH SIDE TO THE FOUR WINDS. AFTER NINE DAYS AND NINE NIGHTS HE SHOULD RETURN BEARING POPPIES FOR EURYDICE AND A NIGHT-BLACK RAM FOR ORPHEUS. THIS HE DID, AFTER THE NINE DAYS AND NINE NIGHTS HE RETURNED AND THE CARCASSES OF THE BEASTS WERE ALIVE WITH BEES, SWARMING IN THEIR RIB CAGES AND HANGING IN SWAGS FROM THE RAFTERS. THIS SPONTANEOUS GENERATION OF BEES FROM THE CARCASSES OF THE SACRIFICIAL BEASTS WAS KNOWN AS BUGONIA. ARISTAEUS'S BEES THRIVED THE GODS APPEASED HE CONTINUED ON HIS TRAVELS AND TEACHING SKILLS THE CRAFT OF APICUCTURE OUT LAND ISLANDS

GEORGICS·IV·VIRGIL

John Burnside

The Fair Chase

De torrente in via bibet;
propterea exaltabit caput

Psalm 109

What we were after there, in the horn and vellum
shadows of the wood behind our house,
I never knew.

At times, it felt like bliss, at times
a run of musk and terror, gone to ground
in broken wisps of ceresin and chrism,

but now and then, the beast was almost there,
glimpsed through the trees,
or lifting its head from a stream

to make us out:
a coarseness on the wind
and brittle voices sifted from the morning.

We tracked the scent through barley fields and hollows,
we followed it into the spinney
with billhooks and sickles,

but nothing was ever there, save the codling moon
and, far in the meadows,
the one field of nothing but grasses

where something had lain,
in a fetor of blood-warmth and pollen,
before it moved on.

Still, we continued;
when one man sickened and died,
another would take his place in the wandering column,

blacksmiths and lawyers, orchardmen,
butchers in waiting,
lost in the fog, or hallowing after the pack,

and all of them friends of my father's; though, needless to say,
in a country like this, the dead have more friends
than the living.

We were the men you saw
on a winter's morning:
cumbersome bodies, shrouded in gunsmoke and cyan,

we went out every day, in every season,
falconers, rat catchers, deerstalkers, whippers-in,
plucking at shadows, purblind, afraid of our dogs,

and if, on occasion, I never quite saw the point,
I was always the first to arrive, with my father's gun,
bound to the old ways, lost in a hand-me-down greatcoat

and last among equals - flycatcher, dreamer, dolt,
companion to no one,
alone in a havoc of signs.

*

One year, the reservoir froze.
I walked out to the centre of the ice
and gazed down through a maze of gills and weed

to where a god I'd read about in books
– sweeter than pine, but stone-hard in his tomb –
lay waiting for a gaze to curse with knowledge.

The ice was clear as glass: I hunkered in
and dared him, from that unreflecting world,
to pull me through, in one bright flash of rage,

no crack, no sudden drop into the cold,
nothing to witness,
nothing to remember.

Minutes I waited; then the others came
and called me back, the dogs a swarm of noise
and worry, old men's

faces in a mist of their own breath
ashamed for my father's sake
and his father before him.

We carried on; I walked off to one side,
and halfway through the white of afternoon,
I slipped away, unwanted, or unnoticed,

taking a road less-travelled through fields and yards
of stunted brassicas and rotting tyres,
strangers in coveralls or leather aprons

stopping to watch as I passed: no hand raised in greeting,
no dog come out
to see me on my way.

That was a foreign country: snowdrifts, then sand,
blotted and kissed with yew-drupes
and windfall holly,

spotted owls hunting for beetles along the hedge,
smoke in the distance, nether roads,
passing bells.

I walked for hours, yet it was light as noon
when I came to a place I thought I had seen before
through a lull in the weather:

nothing to speak of,
a dirt track and sheep in the woods,
and that sense of a burial, under the moss and ruin,

but something was present a few steps into the treeline,
one of those creatures you find in a children's album,
a phantom thing, betrayed by smoke or rain,

or glimpsed through a gap in the fog, not quite discerned,
not quite discernible: a mouth, then eyes,
then nothing.

It lingered a while;
and then, as if it wanted me to play,
it shifted away through the trees – and I followed after.

Crashing through cover, ducking through sumac and maple
it leapt and ran, though never so fast or so far
that I couldn't keep pace

and when I paused for breath, it also paused
and stayed,
as if it wanted me to follow.

I never saw it clear, but it was there:
sometimes the brown of a roe-deer, sometimes
silver, like a flight of ptarmigan,

it shifted and flickered away
in the year's last light
and I came after, with my heavy gun,

trudging for miles
through meadows laced with rime,
working by scent

and instinct, finally
true to myself,
with the body and mind of a hunter

and, by the time I stepped into a glade
candy-striped with light and frosted grass,
I knew exactly what a man should do

in my position – lucky, singled out
by death and beauty for the blessèd kill,
assenting to the creature's dumb assent

to blood and darkness
and the life
beyond.

I took a bullet,
loaded it with care
and aimed with an intent that felt like love,

though I only knew love
by hearsay
and stubborn lack.

No sound, no movement; all the world was still
and not a creature in it
but ourselves,

me taking aim
and the animal stopped in its tracks,
waiting to see what would happen, unafraid,

a deer, I thought, and then I saw a fox,
and thinking I knew what it was
I pulled the trigger.

*

The old days were better for mourning;
better for tongue-tacked women
in ruined plaid

climbing a hillside
to gather the rainwashed bones
of what they had lost, that winter, to the cold,

and men in the prime of their lives,
with dwindled sight,
dreaming all night of that slow white out by the river

where, once or twice a year,
a girl would drown,
pledging her heart to a boy she had mostly imagined.

I remembered the flow country, then,
as the gunsmoke darkened:
I'd go there as a child on Sabbath days,

my father asleep in his church clothes, a fret of chickens
wandering back and forth
at the kitchen door,

a lull in the house and that emptiness high in the roof
as if someone had frittered away
in a summer wind.

I'd go out in my Sunday clothes and shoes
to the shimmer and dart
of sticklebacks threading the light

and search for something I could never name,
the blue of a smile, or the curious
pleasure of the doomed, as they go under;

and that was what I hurried out to see,
crossing the space
to where the beast went down

but all I could find when I got there, standing dismayed
in the stopped air of afternoon, with smoke on my lips
and my heart like a fettered thrush in the well of my throat,

all I could find was an inkwash of blear in the grass
like the fogged stain after a thaw,
and a ribbon of musk

threading away to the trees
and the distance beyond:
no body, no warmth, no aftermath, nothing to prize,

and the night coming down all at once,
like a weight at my shoulders,
settling in waves, till all I could see was my hands.

*

Everyone becomes
the thing he kills
– or so the children whisper, when they crush

a beetle or a cranefly in the dust,
feeling the snuff of it bleed
through the grain of their fingers;

I'd always thought of that
as superstition:
a wishful thinking, how the spirit moves

from one shape to the next
like breath,
or warmth,

infinite kinship, laid down in the blood
against the sway
of accident and weather;

yet out in the woods that night, as I dug myself in
to wait for the day, I felt it in my gut,
a gravity I'd never known before

dragging me down
so it seemed I would cleave to the earth,
the life I had taken

snug as a second skin.
I should have died, if not for that faint warmth
that held me there, unseeing, in a night

so utter, dawn
was like a miracle:
the trees emerging, piecemeal, from the cold,

a snowflake here, then there, then everything
arriving all at once, as I awoke
and, never having slept, began to walk.

I didn't know how far I was from home,
but nothing looked familiar
– not the woods

and not the road I found that afternoon,
dizzy from cold and hunger, hurrying on
through empty yards and desolate plantation,

nothing alive
as far as the eye could see,
only the white of the sky, like a wondering gaze

pursuing me from one field to the next,
from ditch to ditch,
from wall to broken wall.

I walked like that for days. The road led on
through spruce and lodgepole pine, then dipped away
to where a village lay, warmed in a crook

of hills that seemed familiar, suddenly:
a spill of lights and woodsmoke and a kirk
that made me think of something in a book

before I made it out. My dead were there
among the tilted stones;
I knew the market cross; I knew the spire;

but everything was strange, even the house
I came to at the far end of the lane
that passed the abattoir then crossed the brook

and finished at the unclipped cypress hedge
where no one lived next door,
through there were ghosts,

so frail, I only knew them by the sound
the wind made
when it worried at the shutters.

*

Nobody lives
here now, it's only
crows and bees

and every shift
and slant
is an event,

historic
in its void
of mud and wire.

Yet now and again
I have turned
in a falling shadow

and caught a glimpse
of something
at my back,

not heard, or seen,
but felt,
the way some distant

shiver in the barley registers,
before I can think to say
it was never there.

The hunters pass at daybreak, casting
curious looks at my door, but no one is here
to see, as they enter the mist

and disappear.
Nobody lives here now, not even me,
and yet the house is mine – a net of dreams

and phantoms
and that living animal
I followed through the woods: locked in my bones

and calling for the life it must have had
far in the green of the pines, and the white of the snow,
where I am hunting, hunting even now,

hearing that cry
and turning my head,
for an echo.

Pieter Brueghel: Winter Landscape
with Skaters and Bird Trap, 1565

Learn from this picture how we journey in the world
Slithering as we go, the foolish and the wise

We have to imagine the duties they leave behind
for the thrill of the river,
the kitchens and middens, the sheepfolds and clouded byres,
the old folk in their sick beds
mumbling prayers.

The day is bright
and this is their escape
from hardship,
but each has his private hurt, her secret dread:
the man who starts thirsty and tired, his body soured
with last night's schnapps,
then skates out to the bridge at breakneck speed,
away from the loveless matron he's had to endure
for decades;
the woman in blue and grey, keeping pace with her child,
untroubled for now, but never released from the fear
that her husband will catch her wasting his precious time
and beat her as he's beaten her for years,
the moment he gets her home.

At midstream, the children play
with makeshift hockey sticks and, near the church,
a man finds the thoughtless grace
of the boy he was
to glide free
in the very eye of heaven;
it could be simple – paradise foreseen –
but up on the rightmost bank, amid thorns and briars,
someone has built a bird trap from a plank
set on a perch, from which a length of rope
snakes to a half-closed door,
and all around it birds dip from the air,
starlings and fieldfares, redwings, unaware
of any danger.

It seems a fable and perhaps it is:
we live in peril, die from happenstance,
a casual slip, a fault line in the ice;
but surely it's the other thought that matters,
the sense that, now and then, there's still a chance
a man might slide towards an old
belonging, momentarily involved
in nothing but the present and this ochre
sunlight, skating out towards a white
horizon, fair
and gifted with the grace
to skate forever, slithering as he goes,
but hazarding a guess that someone else
is close beside him, other to his other.

From the Chinese

Turn of the year
and a white Christmas turning to slush
on my neighbours' fields,

crows on the high road,
the yard streaked with coal dust
and gritting,

geraniums turning to mush
in the tubs and baskets.

I walk to the end of the road
to ease my sciatica:
ditch water, gorse bones; how did I get so cold

so quickly?

Thaw in the hedge
and the old gods return to the land
as buzzard and pink-footed goose and that

daylong, perpetual scrape
of winter forage;

but this is the time of year
when nothing to see
gives way to the hare in flight, the enormous

beauty of it stark against the mud
and thawglass on the track, before
it darts away across the open fields

and leaves me dumbstruck, ready to be persuaded.

The Bride

And Samson said unto her, If they bind me
with seven green withs that were never dried,
then shall I be weak, and be as another man.

Judges 16: 7

Whatever you should have been, you were never the one
who walked home from the small hours in a veil
of citrus and mariposa, dressed for another
ballo in mascherà,

though someone who looks like you is the woman I spin
from willow and *L'air du temps* for the qualified world
to paralyse with echoes from the Book
of Judges, bowls

of watermark and blood set out to fade
beneath a yellow moon, while you remove
first one ring, then the next, your vows unlocked
and scattered in the dark, *qual pium' al vento.*

John Burnside

Patricia McCarthy: I have called this issue of *Agenda* 'Dwelling Places'. Your poems flow so naturally and magically as if you are simply breathing them out, that they become proper dwelling places for each reader.

'Dwelling places' as such are also very important to you in the corpus of your work. Even in your new collection, *Black Cat Bone*, to be published by Jonathan Cape in August of this year, the persona (presumably yourself) wants a home but is 'stuck in the cage of his bones'. These homes can be made of bricks and mortar, landscape, places in the head or heart (such as when you read contemporary American poetry on arrival in California, you felt you were 'arriving at 'a real home' both 'familiar and strange'), the 'whiteness' of snow or the blank in your mind, even nowhere or the afterlife which you envisage as being incorporated into this earthly life. Can you comment on what seems to be this perpetual need for settlement?

John Burnside: You have raised a few points here. First, I confess that I am extremely happy to hear you say that the poems feel natural, like breath, because that is a central concern for me. It's not something I can try for – not deliberately, anyhow – but I train for it all the time, so any hint of success is gratifying. By which I mean that I tend to place my trust in the made where it feels organic, where it appears to emerge through some natural process. I trust what flows, what emerges, what shapes *itself*.

The relationship of this approach to the way some other poetries work is akin to the relationship between dwelling and a certain way of building. I do not deny that you can build something that lives by its own order, that need not be 'part of the landscape' (actually, every single word in that phrase is just a touch *out*, but I can't think of a better one without using jargon or endless and tedious qualification; I do tend to find myself overusing the phrase 'you know what I mean'). Yet, if I made such a thing myself, I wouldn't trust it. When I first read *Dao De Ching*, that was another occasion where I immediately felt at home – and I've been reading it in my mind ever since on a more or less daily basis. I want to say, though, that I see nothing exotic in it; it's not a case of falling in love with 'Eastern Mysticism', as it were: for me, *wuji* and The Dialectic are close kin, sister paradigms for how the world works, and I feel blessed by both equally.

To get to dwelling, though, it seems to me that there is something quite straightforward going on here. We have Heidegger to thank for understanding that the real problem for humankind is our homelessness – and we have centuries of philosophical thought to thank for the recognition that, if something presents itself to us as a problem, our best answer is to embrace it. It may sound perverse of me, but the truth is that I'd rather follow the path of homelessness to wild dwelling than accept the costly shelter of a certain kind of building – building that displaces, violates and domesticates what some have called, in translation and as a kind of shorthand, *the great spirit.*

In short, the perpetual need for settlement, like the quest for the moment's grace, is necessary because home, like grace, is a temporary, sometimes fleeting thing, and cannot be *occupied* as such. Or not unless one is prepared to lose all hope of wildness and settle for the Authorised Version that mere social life imposes.

PMcC: Another sense of what home means to you persists in the feeling of the travelling towards home being preferable to actually arriving there. Other times 'the place arrives in us'. Is there a T.S. Eliot influence here? In your later poems, too, for example in the long poem 'Le Croisic' from *Gift Songs*, there are quite daringly obvious echoes of Eliot's *Four Quartets*. Can you explain this?

JB: It begins to sound as if my view of home is a bit like some conundrum from quantum physics. Home is there until we try to pin it down, right? Though I think that's partly so. It's like happiness, I think. Let it happen, and you're fine, but you can't *make* it come true.

I am haunted by the Eliot of *Four Quartets*, so I have to be very careful of that. No poet I can think of does time better (though he only does it when he's not *talking* about time, if you see what I mean). How we think of time (or rather, how we inhabit it) is the key question for me. Inhabit it well and happiness of a certain very specific kind will follow. Live in the time of others – the time determined by the clocks and calendars and the decrees of the Authorised Version (also known as 'the world owned by others') – and we lose our *selves*. And I think we know this. It's just hard to admit it, because the others who own the authorised version will occasionally toss us a crumb or a bone to keep us happy. Eliot's greatest achievement, I think, is to make us see how shameful it is to delude ourselves about how time works.

PMcC: This dwelling in 'nowhere' links to your wish, always, it seems to be invisible or to disappear. Even at fourteen, you tell us in your autobiography, *Waking up in Toytown*, you wished to disappear and arrive at 'an unimaginable elsewhere'. This elsewhere must be your perfect 'dwelling place', the point of crescendo in every one of your epiphanies that occur throughout your oeuvre. You tell us further on in your autobiography about 'learning how to vanish'. How does this tie in with your poetry in which you show an authentic self who recounts autobiographical narratives or 'stories'. Isn't there a contradiction here?

JB: I don't think there is. I would say that all the art I particularly enjoy involves a magic act in which the writer, the maker, disappears from the work, leaving a very precise space – a space just sufficient for the reader to echo the artist's vanishing act with his or her own.

So – why do I want to vanish? To experience the world as it is. Not as I have been trained from birth to see it, but *as it is*. Impossible on anything but a short-term basis? No doubt. A worthwhile pursuit? The only one, I'd say, under the present circumstances. It's a cliché, I know, but I don't really see much point in wishing for something else, when you can hanker after the impossible.

PMcC: To what extent is Heidegger a conscious influence in your poetry? His *Poetry, Language, Thought* focuses on dwelling in the sense of our mortal stay or presence on this earth, and on the four divinities of earth, sky, divinities and mortals which co-exist in a primal one-ness, though I am simplifying it all. His concepts seem to fit perfectly with your poetry. Or is this mere coincidence?

JB: No, not a coincidence. I began reading Heidegger in my late teens and struggled for a long time to begin to understand his vision. So his work is central to how I think about the world – but then, so is Marx, Wittgenstein, Sartre, to some extent Merleau-Ponty and Levinas and also Benjamin (with whom I engaged somewhat more recently). Wittgenstein, for example, was an obsession at one time: I remember spending about a year living in a room in Woodingdean, studying the *Tractatus* and living off scraps and milk. I'd been reading it for some time, but I didn't feel I had an overview of it (as it were) so I dedicated myself to it, reading very little else and spending whole days on a single sentence. Sartre, too, engaged me in a very similar way. Though I have to admit that the lifelong engagement has been with Heidegger – the later Heidegger in particular.

That said, I wouldn't use the word 'conscious' when speaking about this. If you do philosophy with care, it doesn't just get into your conscious mind, it affects how you walk about, how you look, how you work in a garden or prepare food. And in a similar way, it affects how we write poetry – not because we consciously think about it, but because poetry comes from our being, which philosophy changes in many subtle but significant ways.

PMcC: Another relevant book, *The Poetics of Space*, by Gaston Bachelard comes to mind when reading your poetry and its focus on dwelling. I recall (upon looking up): 'Not only our memories but the things we have forgotten are "housed" and "the house is a large cradle", including all the houses in our daydream-memories wherein inhabited space transcends geometric space'. Again, is Bachelard important to you, or is it by chance that there are correspondences between your two approaches?

JB: Bachelard is central (not just for that book, but for others, such as *La psychanalyse du feu*, for example) – and I would set alongside him others, like Tanizaki, Soetsu Yanagi, (his masterpiece, *The Unknown Craftsman*, is one I return to time and time again), Leo Marx (*The Machine in the Garden*), James P. Carse (*Finite and Infinite Games*), Annie Dillard and Gary Snyder, for their work on dwelling and what Snyder calls 'wild etiquette'.

But, while it is true that inhabited space transcends geometric space, it's also true that violated space – the space occupied by a dam on a great river, or by a factory farm, or a three-hundred-foot plus wind turbine, *also* transcends geometric space. In fact, it might be said that space and time are – perhaps appropriately – the moral battlefields of our time. We need to honour space so that the beauteous and elegant may grow there – light, shadows, a look, a tree – and we need to reconstruct our notion of time, so we don't just pay lip service to the common knowledge that linear (clock, calendar) time isn't *time* at all, but a convention. We have allowed ourselves to become the slaves of a system that metes out our days to the nearest millisecond, so it can steal from us the places – and the imaginative ways of dwelling in and appreciating those places – those that those who went before us held sacred – for very, very good reasons.

PMcC: In your early work, such as *Common Knowledge* (Secker & Warburg, 1991), and in ensuing collections, including your soon to be published *Black Cat Bone* with its mention of 'venial sin', for example, as well as in your overriding themes of resurrection and redemption, your roots in the Catholic religion that you were brought up in are apparent. How much do you value this influence in your work?

JB: Well, (northern) Catholicism is part of my personal, emotional and spiritual heritage. That is, the iconography is, the imagery and the narratives of a particularly rainy form of Christian dreaming that, for better or worse, I had to work with for a while. Though I have to say that, for a while there, I was engaged in a rather convoluted love letter to Martin Luther. I suppose I would say, if push came to shove, that, at the 'conscious' level (a clumsy notion, but useful shorthand for *some*thing) I lean towards a Daoist view of the world, but my 'unconscious' is a mare's nest of childish and sometimes rather visceral Catholicism.

PMcC: You certainly seem to be preoccupied with the mystery of things, with the spaces between what is known, what you see and what you inquire into.

JB: I'll admit to that. I'm a fuzzy thinking type, and I accept that everything is in flux. I'm making my own small refusal to give in to a certain British pragmatism (which is also shorthand for something, of course).

I also think that there is more to empiricism than trusting the five (why so few?) senses that we have been trained from birth to use, by people with very strong vested interests in having us behave well. That some of those people loved us, or at least had our best interests at heart, is neither here nor there. They were agents of limitation, tasked with ensuring that the doors of perception should remain acceptably muddied.

Not a new notion, in the least. In fact, we know enough about this to accept that, on an almost disastrous scale, we see what we expect to see, what we have been told to see – which preserves certain power structures (political, yes, but also 'moral' and 'intellectual') rather nicely. I don't think that 'I' am going to make any difference, or anything like that, I just don't fancy giving in. Isn't that something akin to healthy scepticism?

Finally, though, I have to confess that I'm also preparing (or trying to prepare) for what is to come, which in my view is the inevitable collapse of a stale civilisation dedicated to the financial enrichment of a few, at the imaginative, moral and spiritual expense of the many. At this stage, *refusal* is significant: to say, yes, you have managed to damage us in countless ways with your fifth-rate socialisation (I won't say education) system and your forced work programmes, but I still refuse to accept that this way of living is inevitable – and I have one useful tool, *Imagination*, with which to continue the mental fight.

PMcC: Your collection *Gift Songs* (2007) was inspired by the Shakers' gift songs and was concerned with a free faith based in the indefinable, nothing to do with dogma. You further this in *Black Bone Cat* where you fuse old and new testaments, 'the Sanskrit of rain', the 'waking at dusk to anatomy's blunt hosanna', 'flesh and blood deities' such as an 'imp' or 'sphinx'; you invoke the old gods who 'return to the land as buzzard and pink-footed goose', who 'fail to love us' because we demand too much of them, and 'outwear' us. This, to me, seems to be an important conscious development which has been gradually happening in your poetry: the synthesis in your work of many religions, including pagan ones, and philosophies.

JB: Maybe it is Catholicism's beautiful – as opposed to one of its many dark – secrets that it preserved, (in a rather cloudy chamber, I admit), wonderful vestiges and DNA traces of the pagan. The Popes told early Christian colonisers to build their churches on the pagan sites and I suppose the intention was to overlay, and so obliterate them. But, under the floor of St Bride's – my first church – I could feel the old Celtic goddess simmering away and, growing up, I think my main task was a kind of DIY and fairly basic re-engineering project, to restore the pagan in my own life, at least, not in the form of residual 'superstitions' and 'folk customs', but as a natural power. At the stage when, like most teenagers raised in a church, I lurched around endlessly spouting half-baked atheist rhetoric, my main objection was the idea of a God with human values and habits – that struck me as an obscenely limited vision, as ugly and crass a way of thinking as a mind that can take a theme from Bach and turn it into an advertising jingle. Those were easy times – 'Man' invented 'God' to fill the gap where 'God' wasn't, because 'Man' didn't want to be homeless and alone in the universe. It takes some of us quite a while to tire of this argument.

Now, though, I tend towards the conclusion that we invent God not, as it were, to replace an absence, but to substitute something we comprehend, or something we can at least deal with, for something we cannot understand. It's the old conundrum of human patterns versus another – not higher or lower, not divine or 'natural', but single, immense and unified – Order, (Dao, if you like). Doubtless, we remake the whole world, not just God, in our own image – which is fine, as long as we recall, from time to time, that *any* order we come up with is only a subset, or a shadow, of that (not human) Order. Our saving grace is that, with a little imagination, we can be wilder and more 'natural' – more pagan, in fact – than we usually allow. Though this has nothing to do with self-indulgence or indiscipline: on the contrary, wildness is a path of rigorous unlearning and lifelong recovery from one's 'education' (socialisation). 'Most people are other people,' Oscar Wilde says. 'Their thoughts are someone else's opinions, their lives a mimicry, their passions a quotation.'

PMcC: This development is furthered by your interest in animism with its attendant spirits and souls that survive physical death and accompany you as ghosts on earth (still evident in your new collection) – so that you are never 'alone' on 'the road to the afterlife'. Can you comment on your moving on from the religion you were born to which is identified narrowly to its adherents as 'the one, true, Catholic church'?

JB: I love the animists – they understand the world so much better than the monotheists and other creatures do. Animism reminds us that it's not enough just to *accept* the cycles of life and death that individuate us; we have to *celebrate* them too. A dark celebration, no doubt, and one in which the tragic has its place, but a celebration nonetheless. Animists say: I assert and praise the world that gave me birth and then, when I die, goes on 'without' me. I can't help coming to the – fuzzy – conclusion that, while the individuated – the named, social person – isn't there in that 'without' state, *some*thing is. *The Gospel of Thomas*: 'Happy is he who already was before he is.'

PMcC: It could be said that you are haunted by your own images which recur throughout your different collections of poetry. Even in the imminent collection *Black Cat Bone*, these same images prevail, used both similarly and differently, as elsewhere, such as the snow, phantoms, the dead, whiteness, cottonwoods and so on; the same influences of art and early black and white film. As if they, like the presences around you, are inextricable from your existence.

JB: They *are* my existence. I would say that this is where the self who 'already was' dwells. There's a 'primitive' belief that, when we need to, we can store our soul – or one of our souls – in a stone or a tree for safe-keeping. That certainly feels like something I can relate to in my own experience. Though sometimes we store our souls in an old movie – real or imagined – where things are a little fuzzy, so they can remain there without becoming contaminated by too forceful a narrative. I have dreamed often of a reel of film, maybe the first film ever made, that still exists but is now so old that almost nothing appears when it's projected, nothing but enticing shadows and flickers. It's like reading old texts – the Pre-Socratics, say, or *The Gospel of Thomas* – where things are suggestive and fuzzy and hugely interpretable. That's where I like to dwell – in that old film. It's always running, somewhere in my mind. Probably it's people walking in snow, or damp woods, but you never really know.

PMcC: Your novels are written in the same poetic tenor as your poetry. Do you see them – the prose and poems – as a single continuum? The group of images I referred to in the question above that recur throughout your work in whatever genre seem totemic or animistic and form a kind of second skin of yours. Is this deliberate or happening at a subconscious level?

JB: Oh, I like that idea. A second skin. That *works*. I'm not really a person who does things deliberately but, then again, I'm a bit sceptical about 'a subconscious level'. In any writer who does both, prose and poetry probably come from the same imaginative set of impulses, but – and this may not be the non-sequitur it seems – it pleases me to note that the method (if I can use such a word) of making prose and that for making poetry are fairly distinct.

How I write poetry – though not how I write prose – is pretty much what Mandelstam called 'on the lips'. That is, I don't begin with a piece of paper and a pencil, I let the poem emerge, allowing it to build up 'in my head' (as it were) and then, when the whole thing – or, for a larger poem, a whole section – has come into being, I write it down. This is the point when I have to worry about interruptions, because if something happens here it can all go wrong, but I can carry a good chunk of poem around in my head for a long time while it is still warm and malleable. The rhythm, the music, holds it there. But there's that moment when things are transferred to paper when everything changes. I don't think about line breaks or anything at the writing down stage, I just scribble it down, on whatever comes to hand, when it's ready. Then I will type it up and think about how it should look on the page – my guiding principle in this being that I see the layout of a poem as a kind of musical notation. For me, a poem in print works in the same way – the print version should allow a reader to hear the poem, as one hears a sonata or a quartet when one reads the score. To this extent, there isn't really a beginning and an end to the composition process – it's something closer to a single, if rather drawn out, event.

Prose is completely different at this level. I think, I reconsider, I make notes; I try, then try again and hope to fail better. If I lose faith, or get interrupted, I don't just walk away. I can circle back around and have another go. I can even decide things for myself – something a poem never lets me do. Now, I don't want this to sound mystical – it isn't. I'm not taking dictation from the Muse, or anything like that. But with poetry, it really is a mystery process that, if the space opens up, it happens of its own accord. I can imagine that space never opening up again – and my never writing another poem. Which is fine. But I can't imagine never writing prose again. It's something I could work at, if it didn't grace me.

PMcC: Do you see the poet's rôle to retain and be in touch with the primitive part of his/herself? You yourself, for example, seem to have a primitive side, as if you belong in some level of your psyche to one of those from a hunter-gatherer society. I noted the hunted 'beast', the hare and the 'oxblood' of a mouth in your forthcoming collection. Also you have a couple of poems on drug-taking which link to the trance states and hallucinations which are part of those primitive societies. The very title of your forthcoming collection, *Black Cat Bone*, is a Hoodoo talisman that confers success, invisibility and sexual power on its owner. Can you enlarge on your interest in this?

JB: Oh, yes. Definitely. I do hope so. And I hope it doesn't seem too digressive to quote Paul Shepard here. Discussing the Fipa of Tanzania, he says, 'Men are dominant. The household, like the society, is the outcome of the superiority of the purposive intellect over the feminine qualities signified by the house interior: heart, passion, privacy, loins, growth and death. Thus the intellect is seen as the dominant member of a duality, arraigned against the manifold nonrational that it overcomes by emergence and change. Speech is the prototype expression of self-activation and rhetoric is valued as an end in itself. "Any culture that insists on individuals committing themselves to one point of duality," says Roy Willis, "exposes itself to the risk that some will find the forbidden option too attractive to be foregone". So, in contrast to the polished, public persona so praised by the Fipa is the savage, interior self, the dark enemy, the wild and wilderness, all that seems resistant to the growth of the known and the corporate village.'

PMcC: Is Jung an influence on you at all? For example, in the long poem, 'The Fair Chase' (from *Black Cat Bone*), the 'beast' that you kill might well represent the dark side of yourself, in Jungian terms: your shadow, and any muse, such as Helen who died young and whom you hardly knew, your anima. Tying in with this, it is interesting to note that in the poem 'Oh No, Not my Baby' in your new collection, a woman 'seemed more song than woman'.

JB: I've not read Jung for years. But then, Jung is a ubiquitous if sometimes unacknowledged influence isn't he? In the atmosphere, as it were. Or in the water. Like fluoride.

PMcC: What other muses do you have? Are they the ghosts and phantoms, 'the limbo people', who preside alongside you, and haunt your autobiography and your poems?

JB: Are they muses? I wonder about that. I am a chronic insomniac, which means I spend a good deal of time consorting with ghosts and phantoms, but they are very good company, much of the time. Sometimes, I fear, I allow myself to think of them as better company than the living, flesh and blood creatures of the day. Which is wrong, in many ways, but those night folk are wonderfully unpredictable and there's an elegance to them that I can't help but admire.

   Though I'm not sure talking like this doesn't over-emphasise the human in the world of my imagination – which is, in fact, populated by all manner of creature, many of them only half-human, and some wholly animal, vegetable or mineral. Not to mention scents, patterns, shadows, numbers. A scent can carry a good deal my way – *L'air du temps*, for example. I have to confess that Nina Ricci is very significant for me – I have no idea why. It's not some simple *psychological* thing – my mother didn't wear *L'air du temps*, for example, while she prepared for a Proustian night out – it's something far less analysable than that. I once went to Chartres and they had an exhibition there of Nina Ricci fragrances through the ages. I stumbled upon it; I didn't know it was going to be there. It was like heaven. Stained glass, catacombs and Nina Ricci. What could be better?

PMcC: Your father, too, is important. Tell us more about him.

JB: My father was a foundling, it seems, who turned up on a doorstep during the General Strike of 1926. Not a good start in life, especially in Cowdenbeath. Growing up, he was passed from one family to another, as far as I can make out, but I don't know much more than that. Naturally, this history made him difficult to live with.

His great gift was that he was a wonderful liar. I sometimes wonder about that. I am suspicious of people when they talk about 'the truth' – often, this just means 'factual', which isn't the same thing at all – and that may be a symptom of my having spent my childhood in a house where 'the truth' was always in doubt and, at the same time, some necessary fiction – the lie that always tells the truth, as it were – was being contrived, from wisps and fragments of event, imagined or 'real'.

I confessed to being a fuzzy thinker, earlier, and I feel that may be an asset, some of the time. Some of the time but not all of the time. It worries me when people say something is true – if they are talking about simple facts, that's fine, but we all know that most things aren't as simply factual as this society wants to make out. We all know that, yet we pretend we don't. We pretend that some uninterpreted 'truth' is possible – and that's a political choice, in many ways. It means some people can be said to be right about things that nobody is ever 'right' about. Who tells history wins power – so maybe the first task is a retelling of history, and a review of what we think we mean by 'truth'. I think Pontius Pilate said that.

PMcC: Is this invisibility you claim to seek – 'as breath spills out and comes, time and again, to nothing – neither echo nor lament', and, 'The only gift is knowing we belong to nothing' (from *Black Cat Bone*) – influenced in any way by the writings of Krishnamurti, or the mystics? Or does the innate inclination or yours to lack a self in a state of nothingness hark back to Sartre and the existentialists?

JB: 'Nothingness haunts being.' Now *that's* a bon mot.

I haven't read Krishnamurti for a long time either. My 'mystic' of choice is probably Simone Weil. The Simone Weil of *La pesanteur et la grâce*, for instance.

Maybe I've been a little misleading though, on the self. It's not my inclination to lack a self; I just don't want to have a fixed self, something to get attached to. I want to live – and die – as fully as I can, and 'self' could well get in the way of that. I seem to recall, too, that 'God is no respecter of persons'.

PMcC: Just as well you say that, since it could be worrying if you were to see your poetry, in future, striving in that more abstract direction, somewhat akin to Laura Riding's aims, to achieve this invisible, unnameable authorship and this nothingness. Is the 'whiteness' in the mind, constantly referred to by you, a place ultimately beyond the world of images and poetry?

JB: I'm not one for striving, which is probably a stroke of luck. I'll go wherever the line takes me. I'm not being flippant, or argumentative, when I say that I don't think of a future, and I don't have aims. I don't think poetry ever has a future, only a present. Which is, I think, a Good Thing.

PMcC: Again in *Black Cat Bone*, you claim, with nostalgia and a sense of loss, that all your childhood seems a fiction. Isn't this one of the tricks of memory, particularly when a past is quite a long time ago? Many of your childhood memories are in Scotland. Does this mean that Scotland, where you now live, has become a fictional territory for you? And if so, does this give you a freedom? Or is it more than that?

JB: Oh, Scotland has mostly been fictional territory for a while now. Not just for me. Though I don't see the protagonist of *Black Cat Bone* as me, or even as an alter ego. A persona, yes, but only a version of me to that extent. For example, I don't believe I'm much given to nostalgia.

The Scotland where I live now is constantly under threat. If you live in the country, it's quite shocking to see how feudal it is still, how big landowners and local worthies are quite happy to lord it over the rest of 'the community'. Rural Scotland is, in many ways, a gift to David Cameron's hideous 'Big Society' notions – it's full of people who would trade everything – the land under our feet, the sky over our heads – for a sizeable enough subsidy or a tariff. I moved to Scotland from Surrey thinking I was going to a place where the rudiments of, or at least a fondness for social justice and a civic sense were still being upheld against the Thatcherite assault (and there are enclaves where such things are still being debated and fought for) but not in the beautiful Scottish countryside where so much of my work is set. There, the deal has been done. Unless we have *serious* land reform – now – the damage will continue to be done. We need much more public ownership / regulation of the land, we need to support sound land management practices (in which wildness plays its part) and we must demand an end to subsidies and 'feed-in tariffs' that take money from ordinary taxpayers and energy consumers and hand it over to big landowners and land management companies. We need environmental policies designed by people who know and understand the issues, not by crowd-pleasing politicians. I'd include all political parties here, including the Greens, whose support for, for example Big Wind, violates at least one of the original pillars of the green movement, (social justice).

Have I strayed from the subject? Maybe. But when I consider these questions, I am reminded of one way in which art 'matters' socially. Any work of art, however small, is a model of order, a world view. It proposes an alternative to the disinformation and lies that permeate the atmosphere we grow up in from infancy onward. The territory of my poems isn't the fiction; it's the map that has all the lines of ownership and privileged pillage that is a fiction – and a bad one at that. And the way I would define 'lie' is exactly that: a bad fiction.

PMcC: Presumably your love of the land, for its flora and fauna, stemmed from your time in Scotland, then later in Northamptonshire. In your forthcoming collection, for example, I notice your detailed knowledge. You use such names as 'alstromeria', 'a pintailed duck'. How careful a study have you made of botany and biology? And how much does science inform your work?

JB: I have studied botany, especially taxonomy, in an 'amateur' fashion. I like the amateur scientists, the ones who operate out of 'pure curiosity'. Some of them work in university labs and get paid; some go on field trips for their holidays – and I have to confess that too many of my 'holiday's have turned into field trips of one sort or another. (The great American fiction writer, Andrea Barrett, is wonderful on this subject, by the way.)

On the other hand, I wouldn't say that using the correct (folk taxonomical) names for a specific flower or bird is *scientific* – it's just accurate use of the language. If I mention 'cotoneaster' or 'arctic tern' in a poem, it's because that is the plant or bird that has to appear there, in that particular representation of the world. Substitute 'holly' or 'swallow' and something else is going on. It's just about giving the metaphor the best chance I can of working in someone else's mind. A reader, or a listener. And I think poetry should value the specific and the actual very highly indeed – because the powers that be are pretty intent on our settling for the generic, and the virtual.

PMcC: Can you comment on what you think of the way you are frequently interpreted as 'a nature/eco' poet and, as such, 'prophetic'.

JB: Ah. Yes. Eco. Can you think of any other term that has been so thoroughly and insidiously colonised in recent years? By all kinds of folk. Eco is the new 'New!' the new 'Fresh!'. Big Wind wants us to believe their turbines are 'green' (they are not, and they draw investment and research away from what could be environmentally beneficial). The supermarket shelves are full of 'eco' products that, while removing a thick coat of grease and grime from your cooker or kitchen counter, still somehow manage to be 'environmentally friendly'. How about 'organic' farmed salmon? How about feed-in tariffs to landowners and businesses for 'renewables' that are paid for by poorer energy consumers, (roughly quoted from the feed-in tariff website: *If you don't put up your own renewables, you'll be subsiding someone else who does*…. That must be heartening to a flat-dweller in Leven or Leicester)? The green 'movement' has become one more refuge for fatcats and windbags – and it needs to be re-taken by deep (dark) ecology thinking.

I don't think we need prophets any more, though (if we ever did). We need action. Three things 'people could do' right now: i) energy: refuse all support to wind energy unless it's wind-and-water, insist on a non-subsidised, *demos-controlled* energy industry and begin serious work on energy conservation and truly sustainable research ii) scrap all subsidies that are not related to the production of quality food, social justice and / or an enriched sensual and cultural and playful life iii) oblige landowners and businesses to clean up the mess they have made of our rivers, land and seas and repossess all violated lands, while working towards a phasing out of land 'ownership' in its present form.

Poetry may well have a place in this work. But only if it's radical. It's not enough to say how pretty cowslips are and what a shame it would be if we lost them. It's a philosophical question, not a matter of public relations. Heidegger says his work is about a search for a new way of thinking. Deep ecology thinking – something my first, rather dismal stabs at 'eco-poetry' characterised as 'dark green' – asks us to put the natural order first, not because we want to 'save the planet', but because it *is* the natural order. Nature offers no home, as James P. Carse once remarked, so humans have to create their own order to survive – their dwelling places, their provisional and constantly negotiated 'homes' – but if they don't do this within the context of that natural order, then disaster will follow, as disaster follows all acts of hubris. Poetry can remind us of this – but, as I say, it's a lifelong philosophical matter, not just a bit of research and a grant application. I still think of myself as a dark green. I'm not in any way prophetic though, and I'm wary of anyone who is. I am also obliged to add that I do not see myself as having succeeded, or contributed to the possibility of success, in any of the objectives – not so far. I travel hopefully, however.

PMcC: As to your mentors – Rilke seems to me to be one (for example your angels relate to his as pagan, earth-bound creatures), as well as Milton, Gerard Manley Hopkins, and James Joyce with his epiphanies similar to your own. We have already mentioned T.S. Eliot. Do you feel their presences when you are writing? What have you taken from poets of the past, and which poets do you admire today?

JB: I'm a bit surprised by your mention of Joyce, but I cannot deny the rest. I'd add Marianne Moore, Montale, Celan, Paz, Saba, Lorca and Jorge Guillén to that list, and there are quite a few others.

 The poets I admire today are many – it's a very rich time for poetry, I think. In the United States, there are maybe too many fine working poets to name. I'm lucky to count a couple of my favourite American poets as friends and they constantly bring other poets to my attention. So last year, while I was on a visit to Michigan, Linda Gregerson handed me a book by Nick Lantz, (*We Don't Know We Don't Know*) which was a *revelation*. Allison Funk introduces me to new work all the time and I feed back my own suggested reading from this side of the water. It's a long and rewarding conversation.

PMcC: In *Black Cat Bone*, further subtle developments can be detected. The usual images are more surreal, more eerie. Childhood memories become like vignettes of an era, recalling Larkin. You take more risks, too. For example, you deal very delicately with a failing marriage which becomes a damaged bird: 'we failed to mend/ that feathered thing we brought in from the yard/ after it came to grief on our picture window.' In another poem, the groom at a wedding (yours?) is 'a corpse-groom with his 'moth-eaten bride' who is 'a marzipan doll'. The occasion is meant to end 'in sugarcraft and satin'. It is this 'sugarcraft' , 'candyfloss' and 'candy', 'the sweetmeat of a heart' or sweetness that is hinted at many times in this collection but is accompanied by a fear that it overlays something sinister. This is reminiscent of the dangerous 'honeydew' poison in Webster's *Duchess of Malfi*. Characters in the poems become more than themselves, developing into allegorical and universal figures such as 'The Well-beloved'. Moreover, you are not afraid to shock such as the poem shrugging off the killing of a woman which is merely like drowning a kitten: 'a little thing', 'it wasn't personal'. There is the 'giggle in the bushes,/ then a shudder'. And the omni-presence of an undefined other who now is perhaps another self: 'someone else is close beside him, other to his other'. There is always the danger that prevails: 'we live in peril, die from happenstance,' a casual slip, a fault-line in the ice'. Not much going for us with our angst.

JB: Well, I see what you are saying here and, of course, I can go along with it – though only up to a point. The wedding in 'Black Cat Bone' isn't mine; it's the dark, reverse image of the mystical marriage that ends all good comedy. It's also the shadow of marriage *as institution*, that grotesque condition in which love becomes a legal contract and husbands and wives are set upon one another as instruments of the overall machinery of conformism and social control. In that model, as I see it, the husband's job is to help render his wife less the woman she could be, just as it is the wife's task to help make her husband less of the man he might have been. My protagonist wants to imagine a free marriage of bodies, souls and minds, but he cannot escape the institution's unspoken rules of limitation and denial, just as he cannot shed his own conditioning, pride and lusts. I would venture to suggest that he is one of the bachelors who strip bare the bride – a process neither erotic, nor liberating. And the bride is a caricature of sugar and spice and seven veils of lace; she's not an actual woman at all.

PMcC: Yet there is the aim (is it yours?) 'to be momentarily involved/ in nothing but the present'. This surely links to the 'paying of attention' in the moment, the emptying of the mind in meditation. And your growing detachment, your speaking with an 'I' that isn't an 'I', in accordance with the words of Wallace Stevens that you quote: 'If the mind is like a hall in which thought is like a voice talking, the voice is always that of someone else'. Are all these adjustments and developments deliberate?

JB: As I said, poetry's concern is with the present. That is, with eternity – which we experience as the 'present moment'. The other stuff – the institutional, the conventional, the socialised spaces – is a matter of linear time, but I think poetry is not. Poetry, for me, is one of the means by which we dispute the imposition of linear time, just as metaphor disputes the notion that the world consists of subjects and objects experiencing one another in various kinds of atomised relationship. Poetry is a heightened way of saying, *Look how thoroughly we are all in this together*, and it's only a seeming paradox that the lyric creates its own, apparently isolated space. It's a space carved out away from the Authorised Version, where the sheer continuum of the world becomes audible and tangible – but it's a space that, while I may have experienced it initially by myself, I shape and craft, after my fashion, for someone else to share.

PMcC: Then there is the question, always, of song. In 'Death Room Blues', a new poem, you write: 'Before the songs I sang there were the songs they came from, patent shreds/ of Babel, and the secret/Nineveh of back rooms in the dark'. The songs, like the undead, mill around you, along with the images that repeat and repeat themselves with no escape.

JB: That sounds a bit ominous. Well, 'no escape' does. And I'm not sure of what answer I'd want to make to this other than to say that 'self' is something we can put on hold for a time (as any meditator knows) but it's not something from which one can escape, not entirely. So what then? There's only a sense of 'no escape' if you want to escape in the first place. I love these songs and images – I even love the nightmares that are my own. I don't want to escape from them.

PMcC: In terms of technique, there is a change in this new collection. There are far fewer stepped lines than in your more recent previous collections; occasional random rhyme, some syllabic lines, some longer lines, and free verse often. Is there a special significance in this?

JB: I don't know. The music of a poem is dictated by the poem itself – all I can do is make mistakes in the transcribing, as it were, and so obscure, or muddle, that music. I hope that doesn't happen too often here, but notation has always been an issue for me.

What I can say is that I've been rereading Marianne Moore a good deal over the last couple of years. That may have had some effect. But I've been going to Saba and Montale too – and Pound. Early Pound, mostly. I can't claim that I've been doing anything deliberate in these forays into familiar and strange territory but most worthwhile things that happen to me happen by osmosis.

PMcC: Has your self-avowed 'apophenia' – seeing patterns or connections in random or meaningless data – been helpful to you as a poet and novelist, or a hindrance?

JB: It's hard to know. The older I get, and the more 'in control' I like to think I am of my mental weather, the more I see that I have never known what it is like to be close to 'normal'. That is, I've always seen the world the way I do and, when that happens, it's hard not to think that other people are only pretending when they claim that they don't see it in much the same way.

I don't mean this flippantly. I find the social world endlessly perplexing, which is probably why artworks – things I make myself, things made by others – play such a central role in my life. Shepard again: 'Art may have begun and continues to serve as the means by which the gap between the natural order and the human order is bridged'. I guess I more or less 'get' the natural order, but the human order – as I presently find it, in the late stages of consumer-capitalism – is something I have to work on.

PMcC: Now I would like to ask the questions Alan Stubbs formulates in his essay further on in this issue of the journal, as they are questions many readers, including myself, would like to ask. You have probably answered a few already. How do you write? Every day? Do you hear a music that decides on the length of each line, and on the rhythm? Do you know where each poem is going to, or what exactly it is about when you begin?

JB: It would be such a pleasure to write every day! I think I probably would if there weren't so many interruptions. I don't want to repeat myself about how 'composition' works for me, but I would just say again that I'm not the deliberate type, I just feel my way, in the present moment, and see where it takes me.

PMcC: Perhaps we should conclude with what would seem to be an important dwelling place for you, as expressed in *Black Bone Cat*, in 'the rollright in the mind', 'touched', as you say at the end of your autobiography, 'with the holy and unexpected blessing of the flyer', singing to us, on and on.

Zoë Brigley

The Potential of Silence:
Re-reading John Burnside's Early Poems
after *A Lie about my Father*

As the epigraph for his memoir *A Lie about my Father* (2007), John Burnside quotes the infamous writer of suspense stories, Edgar Allen Poe, whom Burnside read avidly as a boy. Poe's story, 'The Imp of the Perverse', is famous for theorizing the impulse to self-harm or violence merely because, as Poe suggests, a particular action is something 'we feel that we should *not* [do]'. Burnside quotes Poe's description of an imperceptible force that builds inexplicably: 'a cloud of unnameable feeling' which 'assumes shape, as did the vapor from the bottle out of which arose the genius in the *Arabian Nights*'. Out of intangibility, blankness or silence, something material and powerful can emerge. As Ernestine Schlant notes in *The Language of Silence,* silence is not 'a semantic void' but a 'language […] infused with narrative strategies that carry ideologies and reveal unstated assumptions'.

In Burnside's memoir about his troubled and sadistic father, the genie that emerges from spaces of silence is violence. Burnside says of his father that he was 'one of those men who sit in a room and you can feel it: the simmer, the sense of some unpredictable force that might, at any moment, break loose, and do something terrible'. Silence, however, is related by Burnside too to the powers of the imagination through which he escaped from the painfulness of his family life.

My intention in beginning with this reference from Burnside's memoir is not to create a simple biographical reading; Burnside has said in interview in the Warwick Writers' Series that he 'wouldn't publish poetry if it was about my life' and that his poetry is 'a gift or a letter', which the reader can 'have […] the way you want to'. Burnside's comments on silence, blankness and nothingness in *A Lie about My Father* have interesting parallels, however, with the imagery of his poems. Burnside's début collection *The Hoop* (1988) marks his first attempt to work through his ideas on silence and its potential, and as a book that has been rather overlooked, it is deserving of further attention.

Silence, blankness and lack are redolent in *A Lie about my Father*, which is a memoir about Burnside's family life growing up in Cowdenbeath in west Fife. The book focuses especially on Burnside's father who was abandoned by his parents as a baby, and grew up as 'a nobody: a foundling, a throwaway'. To combat his consequent sense of loss, Burnside's father invented a history and selfhood; Burnside explains the compulsive desire to fill in the gaps: 'He lied all the time even when there was no need to lie'. This blankness is, in part, handed on to Burnside, when his father reveals to him that he once had a sister who died as a baby: 'that her name was Elizabeth, that she had died and that he wished she had lived, and I had died instead'. This appalling revelation initiated a preoccupation with living a ghostly existence and becoming invisible – the man grown from a baby that should never have lived – and describing himself in adult life, Burnside admits, 'I was tired of self'.

This interest in moving beyond ordinary selfhood is clear in the early poems of *The Hoop*. 'Self-' for example exhibits uncertainty about the materiality of identity. The narrator describes the proof of the senses as 'sure', but expressing that self through language is less certain: 'names were all deceit'. The meaninglessness of words is a preoccupation of *The Hoop*, with a lack of naming signalling a kind of disinheritance. In 'The Bounds', Burnside projects this onto physical space in terms of naming and defining place; recalling colonial acts of renaming, he describes 'The old names on the old maps' as 'lists where we find our own words tucked away /into the language of strangers'. Place names are arbitrary and inauthentic, just as the human self is a lack to be filled by invention and storytelling. In 'Self-', the narrator cannot deny his reflection in the glass, but that mirror-image is 'more self than all I was'.

These early poems, which challenge a stable sense of selfhood, anticipate the later collection *The Myth of the Twin*, but the theme of twinning can be seen even in Burnside's early poems. In *A Lie about my Father*, Burnside explains the origins of the twinning idea as resulting from the loss of two siblings as babies. When he was a boy, Burnside imagined his missing siblings as ghosts, and asked his mother, 'Why don't I have a twin?' Burnside was to feel all his life like a kind of impostor and in the silences undetected by others he 'tuned in to a rhythm of an otherworld that nobody else could hear, a whole kingdom of ghost brothers, hidden in the dark' (114). This feeling is explored in *The Hoop* through the poem, 'Brother', in which the narrator describes a shadow self which 'grew beside me steadily, / your mass and volume echoed in my own'. It is through silence that the narrator finds this ghost brother, though it is a silence that chokes and pains him even as it works its empowering 'magic':

My only magic, sharp and hard
like a bone in my locked throat,
I wanted you to catch me unawares,
to step into my shoes and walk away.

The image of the bone in the throat is repeated in 'The hoop', where the narrator finds power through 'silence [that] hardens in my throat like bone'. The inability to speak and withdrawal into silence signals, however, the possibility of transformation. In 'The hoop', this means the potential to 'shout' a devil or 'breathe the angel out', so silence has demonic or holy possibilities. The strongest desire in 'Brother', however, is simply to disappear, to become part of that silence, while the shadow-self lives out the narrator's life.

In this state of non-being, Burnside's narrators are listeners who anticipate the consequences or potentialities of silence. In *A Lie about my Father*, Burnside describes his boyhood visions of things beyond the surface of everyday life: 'something appeared: not spirit, not flesh, but something between the two, like the faded stain of blood and salt on the sleeve of a fishmonger's coat'. As the blood and salt suggest, silence often precedes violent acts, in this case the butchery of the fishmonger. This kind of silence is negative in that it hides the more brutal aspects of communities which society prefers to ignore. Burnside explains: 'Everything stayed hidden [...] it was all secret – known by anyone who cared to know, but unacknowledged, like a priest's feverish brightness around adolescent boys, or the beatings Mrs. Wilson endured on those Saturdays when Dumfermline lost at home'.

The idea of silence as a prelude to brutality contrasts to the more traditional poetic theorizing of silence as contemplative, giving rise to epiphanic moments. In 'Keeping secret', Burnside explains that 'Whenever a silence fell I knew it was there // for a purpose' and the poem concludes with the consequences of silence: the narrator as a voyeur 'watching a stranger do terrible things in the shadows'. 'Silence is possible' suggests the potential for a more positive kind of silence; the narrator has been 'a listener for years' seeking 'silence, like a glove, / the perfect fit you always hoped to find'. The poem, however, ends with the bleak, destructive silences that dominate *The Hoop*:

and what could you find but the hard quiet
of huddled swimmers in the riverbed
or the casual hush of abattoirs
after the thud of a bullet nobody heard.

Although this thought begins itself as a question, the lack of a question mark denies the possibility of ever finding the positive silences sought at the beginning of the poem. What is found instead are silences of death (the drowned bodies), silences after butchery (abattoirs) and silences of murder gone unpunished (the bullet unheard).

This kind of silence is related to Burnside's ideas of 'darkness'. Contrasting with the regenerative silences of the blank page, unspoiled sheets and snow, there are silences of darkness, the chasm and self-negation. The silences of darkness or blackness are empowering, but are fatally linked to brutality and violence. In *A Lie about my Father*, Burnside explains how his father embraces darkness 'like some brother he would rather have done without, but could not turn from his door; and 'over the years, it came to possess him'. Burnside's idea of darkness parallels Poe's thoughts on the power of perversity, and Freud would probably have labelled it the 'Death Drive'. Burnside writes in 'The hoop' how 'dark is welling up', its destructive energy filling the narrator's hands with 'freezing seed'. Exploring 'my blackness at the core', the narrator tries to 'spell things out', but 'from utter silence every word is strained.' What is clear, from Burnside's comments in *A Lie about my Father*, is that this dark, destructive power is 'Continuous in the life of everything [...] an inescapable fact of existence'.

Like his father, Burnside embraces destructive energy as 'a brother', and he describes a shadow-self which appears alien, foreign and unfamiliar to his everyday life. In *A Lie about my Father*, Burnside conjures a 'dark face' or 'a stranger' within himself, 'a primal energy that carries me forward when nothing else will'. Like the covert forces of the unconscious, this shadow-self represents chaos; it 'thinks less of danger and propriety than I ever have or will, feels a cool and amused contempt for the rules and rituals by which I live, the duties I too readily accept, the compromises I too willingly allow'. The sense of foreignness within the self, described by Burnside, recalls the philosopher Julia Kristeva who describes the frightening possibility of there being a strangeness – an unknowable quality – within ourselves. It is this fear that creates animosity, rage and cruelty directed at strangers or foreigners around us. Kristeva argues, however, that those who embrace their own strangeness – the foreigner, the depressive and the poet – can achieve a kind of creative and productive *ekstasis*, a state of going beyond oneself. Burnside seems to agree with this idea in *A Lie about my* Father, when he writes about his childhood visions. In a state of selflessness, Burnside discovers 'something angelic that had chosen a shape I couldn't quite believe in, coming out of a wall or a door and filling my room with brightness and delicious fear'.

Though silences can be frightening and terrible in Burnside's poetry, there is a possibility of reaching the sublime or epiphanic through silence. The poem 'Silentium' explores isolation and wordlessness, but the silences here are of 'snow piled against the hut door' and 'winter afternoons', rather than the dark silences that precede brutality and violence. In a religious sense, 'Silentium' refers to a state of faultlessness or perfection, a condition desired by the narrator. He describes the 'wireless behind the net / window, keeping its own counsel', and admits 'I wanted to be like that: alone / and listening'. The narrator keeps up a vigil by the fire 'guarding / a thin yellow flame', and, going outside to fill the coal scuttle, he finds a brief moment of liberation and beauty. He describes how he 'would stand in the dark a moment, / the scullery glow at my back / and my face to the wind'. It is a stance of defiance, freedom and self-determination. On the threshold between home and beyond, between the warmth of the scullery and the forces outside, the narrator loses himself in the beauty and silence of the moment. This only seems to confirm that silence can be precious, sublime and healing. As Fyodor Ivanovich Tyutchev states in his own 'Silentium': 'Live in your inner self alone / within your soul a world has grown.' This inner life combats the dark silences loaded with expectation of violence, and offers the possibility of redemption from the imp of the perverse, the frightening darkness within ourselves.

Further Reading
Burnside, John (1988) *The Hoop*, Manchester: Carcanet.
Burnside, John (2007) *A Lie about my Father*, Saint Paul MN: Graywolf Press.

Philip Pass

The Plight of Dwelling:
'Settlements' and the Making of Home

In an essay entitled 'Strong Words', contemporaneous to John Burnside's award-winning poetry collection, the *Asylum Dance*, he outlines the manner in which he perceives contemporary poetry to be too often the choice of a 'crude' form of '"message"', one adverse to nuance and subtlety. Faced with such general preference for the overt, John notes that he is 'dismayed' by the 'common misapprehension' that in order to have 'political or social interests or usefulness', directness is required. Diverging from such a conception, he considers his poetry to be a more delicate and complex exploration of our place in the world, one which poses a series of questions surrounding what it means to dwell:

> The making of a world – of *home* – is determined by the spirit which the participants bring to the process. The right way to dwell is to constantly examine the making of home: where and what are its bounds? how do we belong there? what do we consume, and what do we have the right to consume in this place?

As he notes, the 'just answer to these questions can arise only from a spiritually rich life', and it is thus the place of poetry to engage with this concept of the spirit, of what such an existence would mean. In examining this plight of the 'making of home', and of how to ensure a spiritually rich life, John constructs a poetics that is 'the choice of a quest, as it were, as opposed to a settlement', an '*inventio,* by which we create ourselves from moment to moment'. Thus, in 'Settlements', one of four longer structural pieces which shape *Asylum Dance*, it is precisely this topic of the plight of dwelling, of the choice between quest and settlement, which forms the focus of the poem.

Comprising four sections, the first part of 'Settlements', 'A Place by the Sea', charts the problematic nature of dwelling and of home. As John notes

> [...] what we think of as home
> is a hazard to others
> our shorelines edged with rocks and shallow
> sandbanks
> reefs
> where navigation fails.

The hazardous nature of such a landscape is captured in the form with which the poem appears on the page. Its frequent indentations, and the discursive quality of the work's void space, depicts the sense in which the language from which home is created is assailed by the whiteness that borders denotation: the pressure of the surrounding emptiness which leaves words such as 'sandbanks' and 'reefs' adrift like the phenomena they describe; a hazard to both self and other. Thus the pagination of the first section – its indents, line-breaks, and stanza endings – reflects the jagged, liminal space of the shoreline, in turn capturing the shaping force which the landscape has upon the possibility of dwelling. Even as it shelters, home is also a space which excludes and denies, leaving those who cannot navigate its complex currents to be washed out to sea, caught in 'a line of creels' a 'mile from land'.

Even for those able to safely traverse its tides, home is still a difficult harbour to sustain, its viability shaped by the spirit of its participants. Within each house that comprises such a community, the same conflict is waged, between quest and settlement. Each home is thus a microcosm of the complex relationship of community, shoreline and sea; the problem of dwelling and of the other, charted in the poem's third section, entitled 'Well'. As John observes:

> – there's more to the making of home
> than I ever expected

Rather than the shared objects which surround the couple functioning as a material embodiment of what holds them together – 'the house' and 'our stilled bed' – they are instead the detritus of a settlement, the burial marker of a quest:

> the book you have left face down
> on the kitchen table,
> the tangle of hair in the brush, the litter of clothes

The pathos of this image, its isolation, helps to remind the reader that, as John observed in his essay, our '"outward" life is about a certain form of limitation, a defeat of sorts', which comes from the surrender of our 'essential' and 'peculiar gift to live as spirits': the abandonment of the uncertainty and doubt of a quest, for the stability and surety of a settlement which does not question its own viability, its own right to consume. Thus, for its participants, 'the making of a home' becomes 'a process of excavation' within such material, of trying desperately to find

something within myself to set against
the chill of the other,

a means of clinging to the openness which characterises a spirit; in spite of
the crushing burden of a 'painful gravity' that 'comes of being settled on the
earth', cast, by connection, into an existential form which is 'unseasonable',
'stubborn', and 'everyday'.

Yet within the poem, dwelling is not simply a surrender absent of the
potential for spiritual affirmation, a theme explored within the third section
of the work. Beneath the grounds of home itself, a spiritually nourishing
life-force remains present, if buried: a wellspring 'deep beneath the house'
which seems to speak of 'the sifted heart of matter.' Such is the comfort of the
everyday, however, that even when such a source is discovered, it is merely
'tasted for an hour' then 'put away' again, before the occupants return once
more to the insulating interior of their home, 'coming in'

to all they knew, immersed in the quiet purr
of radio, those voices from the air
bleeding in through swallow-songs and bees
to make them plausible again

allowing the participants to surrender themselves to the security and stability
of a home which remains a settlement, rather than a quest. Such ephemeral
moments of grace cannot compete with the plausibility of the radio, and nor
can they form the shared basis of a home within a world which distrusts such
phenomena. Instead, they merely ensure 'that the world':

seems strange
on nights like this

when we lie with the ghosts of ourselves.

Yet, in spite of this seeming lack of significance, such moments remain a
troubling force, shattering the first person plural of the community, and the
couple, which governed the majority of the poem's opening section. Such
unity is instead transformed into the first person singular of the isolated self
who is alone 'when I turn / to sleep'.

Within the poem, such moments thus become a rupture for both the self
and the reader in the plausibility of the everyday, a point of access to fleeting
moments of grace: indications that an authentic form of dwelling remains
possible, even from within a life of compromise. However, as the epigraph of

the poem observes, 'God answers our prayers by refusing them', and rather than providing the basis for a new form of transcendence, such moments of grace inevitably remain merely 'an atmospheric trick':

> a common miracle that finds us out
> alone in attic rooms

Thus, while the fourth section begins with a visit to a Pictish holy site – 'the spirit of the place' embodying their supposedly close connection of language, environment and dwelling – for the modern self of the poem such 'holy ground' is 'barely recognised', and remains separate from the making of a home. Rather than forming the basis for a spiritually conscious community, such unverifiable moments of grace, which puncture the plausible skin of the text, are instead experienced alone. While the first three sections of the work debate the tension between quest and settlement, the final part, 'What We Know of Houses', thus poses the question of what is left for those who would try and dwell as something alchemical, spiritual, beyond what the poem terms as the 'painful gravity' that 'comes of being settled on the earth', and of 'holding what we love / in common': a settling which always takes 'for granted' our place in the world, and which never questions what it means to dwell.

While for John 'we become most aware of ourselves as spirits when we love', ceasing 'to be conditioned social existences', and instead 'emerg[ing] into being', as 'Settlements' shows, love is also the very same force which can bind the self to a life of compromise and of plausibility. As he observes, within such a connection, driven by such needs and longings:

> [...] we go on digging when it seems
> there's nothing else to find – or nothing more
> than ghosts and unanswered prayers –

Just as the shoreline connects, separates and endangers the other, so too does love bridge and create a sense of both connection and distance, stretching out between self, couple and community:

> redeemable   inventive   inexact
> and capable of holding what we love
> in common
> making good
> with work and celebration

As John observes, within such a dwelling which denies the possibility of grace, what remains is 'not the better part' which 'we hoped for', but merely the 'old need' which 'keeps us strong': the longing to love and to be loved in return, to be part of a union and a community that can hold what we treasure in common; even if the price for such connection leaves the self hungering for 'a rhythm in the light', a tantalising glimpse of the heart of matter beyond the artificiality of walls and flagstones.

In depicting the choice of a settlement over a quest, and the embrace of a form of love which, predominantly, is that of a mortal and not that of a spirit, John's poem opens a dialogue with the second epigraph to the *Asylum Dance* collection, taken from Marianne Moore's 'The Paper Nautilus':

> like the lines in the mane of
> a Parthenon horse,
> round which the arms had
> wound themselves as if they knew love
> is the only fortress
> strong enough to trust to.

Though love, within 'Settlements', can also become a mighty fortress, keeping those it connects 'strong', and providing the ground upon which the self and other can become plausible, and share their lives with those who surround them, it is also a grave within which they bury their potential to live as spirits. Within the world the poem portrays, love remains a compromise: an existence of loneliness in spite of community, and of loss despite connection. Just as the very language which connects contains the same words which alienate – a shoreline both greeting and denying the other – so too does love, like the ocean which dominates the poem, both nurture and destroy.

In the world of 'Settlements', within its nuanced portrayal of complex, everyday, relationships and community, the life of a spirit and its quest remain, for the self, merely 'the echo you do not hear, when I stop to listen'. As such, they are phenomena that only manifest in the scattered moments of grace when plausibility fails, and when, rather than 'redeemable', 'inventive' and 'inexact', the self is instead felt to be 'unseasonable', 'stubborn' and 'everyday'. Within such an absence of spirituality, the plight of dwelling within the poem is that a home has been constructed, a settlement, whose 'painful gravity' ensures that, rather than doubt and uncertainty, all that remains for the self is to

> [...] drive back through the slowly dimming fields
> to quiet rooms
> and prayers that stay unanswered.

Gemma Green

Infinity and Beyond

I met John Burnside in the summer of 2008 when he led a series of poetry workshops for the Dartmoor Arts Project in Devon. I'd not read much of his poetry at this time and had built up a picture of him, as we all do with many people, from his name alone. The image was one of a ruddy cheeked, well-worn, well whiskey'd Scotsman of about 60. As it turned out, he looked a lot more like a cherub and although the whisky part was right, (well, red wine actually) he came across as a man of great sensitivity with an air of otherworldliness and also that thing of great rarity, a great poetry tutor.

Some people are transformational in your life. Not always those closest to you, or even people you are particularly connected with, and for me it was John Burnside. That summer of 2008 was a turning point for me, both in my personal life and in my poetry writing. Burnside brought in the work of such writers as John Berryman, Bernard O'Donoghue, David Harsent, Mary Oliver and led us in meditative exercises, brainstorming (which bordered on telepathy), and lateral thinking. By the end of the week I had pushed my poetry beyond its limits.

Burnside is a prolific writer with several books of poetry, not to mention novels and non-fiction books under his belt. When I first approached this article, I borrowed all his poetry collections out of the library, put them down on my desk with a hearty thump and set about reading them in order. With hindsight, I would not recommend this. Reading any poet's work from 'start to finish' is probably overkill, but in particular with John Burnside. His work is anything but chronological and if you dip in and out of Burnside's work, your reading experience will be all the better for it.

Burnside's poetry has no boundaries. There's no way into it and there's no way out. It takes down walls or at least makes them transparent and feels around the cracks in between the more pedestrian elements of the world to the elusive 'otherness' of things. Unlike many of the poets and philosophers of our times, he appears to have no difficulty merging physical and spiritual worlds and much of his poetry gives you the feeling that he has found a hole through to another dimension.

Life's little questions do not appear to keep Burnside up at night. His work moves like a medicine man weaving through the village, tearing open existential truths and leaving the entrails beautifully scattered for us to pick over. *The Light Trap*, shortlisted for the 2002 T S Eliot prize, is littered with great examples of this, in particular the exquisite poem 'The Gravity Chair' (p.30):

I used the think old age would be like this:
the afternoons more sudden than they are
in childhood, and the snow against the glass

The image of the snow and the suddenness brings to mind MacNeice's masterpiece 'Snow,' and yet Burnside gives it the transcendental treatment, probing right to the heart of human mortality, describing old age in the end as

adapting to the pull of gravity
by shifts and starts, till something in the flesh
– a weightedness, a plumb-line to the earth –
revealed itself, consenting to be still.

In human relationships too, Burnside treads the line between concrete and abstract colours of human emotions. His collection *The Asylum Dance*, which won The Whitbread Prize shows his flair for this in the title poem, where the narrator gives an account of the annual meeting of a small townsfolk and the inhabitants of the local asylum:

We went there for the dance: a ritual
of touch and distance, webs of courtesy
and guesswork

The narrative remains tight throughout while at the same time rendering a luminous quality to the experience that is Burnside's trademark. He touches on unlikely pairings, friendships formed in adversity and ends the poem describing the participants'

faces melting, one into the next
as if they were all one flesh, in a single dream,
and nothing to make them true, but space, and time.

Burnside's latest collection, *The Hunt in the Forest*, named after Uccello's famous painting, explores the theme of loss. Like many of Burnside's collections, you get a feeling of walking through a forest when reading it, the notion being that you are exploring, walking without a path, and often on unsteady ground. Death, decay and rebirth are all examined, but again with a unique slant. The first poem in the book takes place in a swimming pool, a seemingly synthetic setting for Burnside. The narrator talks about a time when he dived into a public swimming pool and did not emerge for some time, as his cousin looked on:

51

even he took a scare, that afternoon
in the public baths, when I didn't come up for so long,
lost in the blur of the pool as he stood at the rim.

As with many of Burnside's poems, the magic occurs in his rendition of what is recalled, and is now lost. Bringing the narrative into the present, the narrator says,

Now, when I swim, I remember what failed to happen:
the body I never found in the glimmer of chlorine,
the casual ascent and the gleam of my cousin's approval;
I dream of the absence I missed and the shiver of longing
that played on my skin for as long as it took me to
    surface

Burnside's talent lies in absences, in loss, and that which slips away; the things that elude most ordinary folk and even extraordinary writers. His work is a constant reminder of the frailty of the human condition, revealing the wide open spaces between what we are able to know and touch, and what lives and breathes invisibly amongst us.

Robin Robertson

for John Burnside

Wildering

The overnight fall has covered the fences.
A perfect white,

the depth of an eight-year-old child.
Impossible to tell now

were you to run out into it,
whether it might be a field or a lake;

if the ice will hold
or, if it is solid ground after all,

if that field might be armed
with stakes and barbed wire

and, either way, with the coming storm,
whether anyone will ever notice the marks

of that line through the snow,
or miss you till the thaw.

James Simpson

The Untenanted Room

for John Burnside

Gods lived here once
and men;
great works
scraped the sky
but the roofs fell in;
ripe skins burst
like a carcass bloated
in the sun;
even the flies have left
turned and run.

Gods lived here once
and men;
but the walls crumbled,
roads ruptured;
how quickly the gold lipped
turn grey;
broken into rubble heaps,
wall braces, iron piling
mangled, contorted to the abstract;
someone laughed here once
on this street corner;
saw the moon
in a pale day
and smiled;
all have passed away.

Here is the empty place;
the untenanted space
where no dweller dwells.
We are that place,
not properly inhabited;
swept clean, adrift, cut off;
hung on the grid of numbers.

Peter Dale

Second Comeback

for Mill Stone

Lethean, if you return
you'll have no memory
but I shall.
'To whom it may concern'
– that how you'll home on me?
Oh, salutations.

Who am I? You'd get it wrong,
your own identity
wiped to all-hallows.
But I remember scar-long
what you have been to me
behind face value.

You loved all that I was?
– Wanted it vacuum-packed,
immalleable,
stamped with a rugged cross.
Your last gasp failed in the act.
So valedictions:

Lethean, you can't return.
Your memory has gone.

Exile

(An extract from the unpublished novel *Landlocked*)

My lovely country is a land-locked realm.
The mountains thwart the child imagining seas,
the troughs of those vast breakers, evergreen trees,
no pen nor print could ever overwhelm.

Now captious Ahab's bearing holds the helm,
the land is ice-bound, white horses topped with snow.
Snow-bodies freeze on floes that do not flow.
Banned is my language – uttered still, though seldom.

Its culture threads back past paper, birch-plaque, vellum.
I will not speak Ahabic; the mother tongue
is mine, and mine its voice: it must be sung.
Mobius dicta I am, and most unwelcome.

An exile in a land unspeakable,
I watch, I warn; my beat is littoral.

Tim Liardet

A Portrait of my Grandfather in Drag

When all those who do not wish to play with him are left at home
he steps into the storm, the free-for-all, of chromosomes;

the future's a swarm of heat in the road – he so rouge-obsessed
we lumbering oafish boys might fear we'll never get to exist;

we fear he'll never get to fill the shoulders of his coat, or fit
the belt that here would wrap around him twice like a straitjacket;

he's an identity, he seems to imply, under construction
but for the time being is bits of self flung in all directions:

in Richmond, though, in what might be Nineteen-Twenty-Three,
or Four, it's lip-gloss, fan and feathers and bits that fly away

as the lippy girl, who so disturbs me, steps out of him to reveal
the forces perched precariously on that abyss-edge of stool –

I'm disturbed but curious and, through the magnifier, trace
the last centimetre of a hair that separates the uncle from the niece

and the niece from the angels. The flash explodes in the dark
and between him and it a daylight of reciprocated shock.

Look in any encyclopaedia. *Gender's* a river in Noord-Brabant,
a gong struck in Javanese gamelan music and the agreement

of noun and pronoun, but tonight, says grandpa in his billowy silk,
the rest is so much glazed and so much slippery talk.

The Dark Age

By the time the second plane blew up
all he knew was he was one of a new race
entering a new age, in need of water:
the cloud of ash bulged between skyscrapers

that seemed to lean closer and he knew
his brother was there at the source of it –
so he stopped, he did the strangest thing,
he took off his railway-worker's coat

to improvise a street-bed, he thought of
unlacing his boots but recalled how a toe
poked through his sock-hole, then turned the coat
inside-out with the satin to the light

and rolled it up slowly, put his head
to the pillow he had made – his brother,
he knew, was at the source of the cloud
so he lay himself down exactly where he was

there in the street, tucked up his knees,
smiled, or wore a face that nothing could name,
then slept as the snowfall of ash, petal
for petal, covered him and everyone else.

Deleted Scene (The Frog)

The terror lived in the shed, we knew. It was the buckled mirror
propped in the depths, in which the frog grew smaller and smaller;

poor frog, it dried up so slowly in our tin's evaporating wet –
too unthinkable to touch, too much to prod or handle, let

alone to sluice it with water. It was like a little old man –
a little old man with an old man's withered fingers and hands

that disturbed us to our hair-roots, while the spider on stilts of hair
stumbled over the nape of our necks and made us both shiver.

And I left you crouched at the door, brother, when the shed's roof-felt
so pressure-cooked the terror, and grew so hot, it'd all but melt;

I left you crouched there once I had, considering how to, stepped
through the speckled sheen of frog and mirror in one step.

The step was long, and now you're dead, I find myself wanting to ask
for some primitive forgiveness – against the slit of sky, cirrus-flashed,

you were abandoned to a space less than half a metre square
and circled yourself repeatedly, or strained into the dark from where

it was always high August and the door-slit bulged a brilliant fog
out of which you stooped and grew smaller, face to face with the frog

that looked straight through you to where more than sun bulged in;
that was just the shape of its frog-mouth, I swear it, and nothing like a grin.

The Peacemaking

Your son, father, your elder son leant over
your eyebrows which rose slowly to meet:
from the open bedroom door I could overhear
him whisper: 'I'm *sorry*, I'm *sorry* …' You splayed your feet

then lifted a deathbed finger in a gesture
of not-having-heard-a-word, then puffed your cheeks. The slit
in the blown blind shed light across your chest
as if actually cutting you in half – a perfect cut

made between gusts from the outer world.
These were the words he spoke to you, the very last,
and now he's dead, and the monkey tree which cast
the family home underwater is felled:

the stump's all sprouting foliage, as if iron had blood;
as if blood were the peace that was never made.

Ian Parks

Mill Bank

Incongruous in your cocktail dress
you walked out from the wood.
Children playing under the stone bridge

were startled for a moment then went back
to wading through reflections, spools of light.
And there you were – black-laced, diaphanous –

stepping over stones and tangled roots,
uncertain in your city shoes.
The place had been important once:

a mill, a mill-dam and a packhorse track
that led us up and over a sheered bank.
I stopped myself from picking out

the brittle bits of branches from your hair.
Then, as we climbed the steepest hill
away from the complexities of shade

past chapels, stacked-up houses, dry-stone walls
I had no words to match the randomness
of what had happened or was happening.

Incongruous in your cocktail dress
you seemed to be the spirit of the place:
encountered, not forgotten, always there.

Josephine Balmer

Aetiology

No more heroics. No more gloss or lexicon.
As Troy festered like a freshly-opened wound,
there were new stories now, for half-schooled
common soldiers, for one illiterate Light Infantryman:
I saw him walk the dappled path just ahead of me

golden-haired, whistling, his job to collect the water,
haloed by the sun as if nothing could fail or falter.
Suddenly that fair hair was scarlet, jerkin soaked,
he wheeled round, smiled, as if at some secret joke,
half his head blown away and still humming 'Tipperary'...

No Hero then, but an early-flowering Hyacinthus:
another blonde youth for the healing god to weep,
inscribe on blood-stained petals the scented script of grief.

Gemini

after Burnside

Every year, to the day, my mother has told it:
the washing pegged-out on a June afternoon
like a field-hospital tent, the scent of grass for gas
and air, gull shriek for surgeon's instruction;
pushed from the womb by my own dark image,

half-formed, misshapen, already suffocating.
Later the midwife gave instructions to burn it,
folded in brown paper like a forgotten parcel
but in the shell-like garden which had given me life
my father tenderly took the other out for burial.

This year, for the first time, there will be no story
just memory's fossil, the feathered trace of her
flesh in ours; a small heap of earth another family
will long ago have turned over or disturbed
to plant poppies, or roses, pale as new-born skin,

petal linked to petal, that perfect symmetry,
unfolding in the sun like the myth of the twin.

Andy Brown

The Departure

i.m. Dereke Leslie Brown

i

Shrunken, gaunt, you lay like a saint
penitent in his ruined sanctuary,
strewn with relics, crumbling slabs.
The broken past lay deep inside
the hollow of your heaving chest
asking to be repaired with each
defiant rasp. Holding on, I told you
all about the birch tree in *my* yard,
reminded of the birch tree in your own
we sat beneath in summers long before
caution made you cut the giant down.
The present recedes into the past
the way a landscape shifts: the browns
and greens so close-up; distant blues.

ii

You were heading to your distant city,
with that *plenitude of bliss*; the peace
that comes of self-command, or maybe
just acceptance, as at the end of an illness,
no longer lost in delirious dreams, staring
fixedly at nothing – what mystics call
the contemplative state. You were gone.
 But for those of us who had to stay
'getting away from earth a while' was no
option – the real and evanescent world
keeps coming back to touch, and back
to mind. It erupts through skins, the thin
veneers with which we keep it covered:
like the face rising from the pool before us.

The Last Thatch

for Thomas Lynch

The sun had dried the haggard to a crust,
whilst, up on Riley's roof, they hammered slates.
The donkey's hooves were puffing up the dust

as we listened to the roofers' repartee – they cussed
each time their new apprentice made mistakes.
The sun had dried the haggard to a crust.

'You need to watch your bloody work. A hefty gust
might see you boost the unemployment rates…'
The donkey's hooves were puffing up the dust

below, tired of the heat and apparently nonplussed
that soon he'd face the derby's starting gates.
The sun had dried the haggard to a crust.

Racing themselves, the roofers said they must
'Get the whole shebang finished before eight',
when donkey hooves would puff the racetrack dust.

The thatch was gone; the new slates 'more robust';
the starter's gun discharged on real estate.
The sun had dried the racetrack to a crust
where donkey hooves were puffing up the dust.

Zoë Brigley

Daughter

'I wanted you to catch me unawares,
to step into my shoes and walk away.
              John Burnside, 'Brother'

Something is stirring in the old wheelhouse
where I listen at night under mutters of snow:
the moan of salted wood against crippling waves,
and the rock and ebb of a cradling crib.

A train groans at the end of the line as it turns,
its pistons silent but braced for revolutions.
Between the ancient stones of the wheelhouse barrow
darkness nests, stubborn as cement or clay.

Something black is crossing the hillside snow:
a dark orb on the white wing of a butterfly,
a beaded owl eye nesting in creamy feathers,
a black beetle hunting on the face of a clock.

In the wheelhouse of the dark, my ghost daughter
stirs, enters my heart through black and briny blood
that beats in spasms. She's inside me somewhere
in a place I can't reach, like seabeds where no sound has been.

Behind the Looking Glass

'Although the mirror watched me when I moved […] I never failed in peeling from
the glass'

John Burnside, 'Self'

She tries not to remember the things he did to her,
never a sound, so she is watching it behind glass.
Her cheek presses against the pane, her breath
fogging the window, while something scrambles
outside in the dingy yard; the light switch
twitches on. Certain things do come back to her.
How on the way home from the pub, her legs
collapsed beneath her. How she was so light
that he carried her home, not for love's sake,
but to turn her over and over in his hands.
How whenever he left her, he would kiss
her forehead while she pretended to sleep
and he pretended not to notice. How sometimes
he held her, his fingers making long strokes
along her golden head. How she wandered
the yard at lunchtime pulling her sleeves down
over her wrists where he'd hurt her.
How she realized at last that not even love
could justify this, that no affection could, not ever.
Still, in the glass, she sees her own mouth,
opening and closing and silent as a fish.

Jaime Robles

Threads

'Threads of Feeling'
exhibition at the Foundling Museum, London 2011

i

Foundling 2275, a boy

This Silver Ribbon is
desired to be preserved as
the Child's mark for distinction

This ribbon binds but also reaches,
observes the shortest distance between me and her,
maps the call of a bird –
tinsel and silky: each stitch a feather.

The bleak streets are forested with pigeons and magpies,
starlings eke out a regime of seeds and pebbles,
dung and bitter water – their startling sheen
like the glitter of a tooth, or light caught in the corner of an eye.

Mama, I would have said. Manna.

Foundling 220, a girl

… pains should be taken to convince them,
when young, that subordination is
necessary in society …

How can I remember what was never forgotten?
I arrived here festive, sleeves blue and white strip'd cotton.
My wrists cuffed in white linen and purple flowers.

Catlike and stealthy, a narrow silk ribbon coils, pink,
through my dreams, recalling luxuries of breast and mouth.

The darkly wooded staircase winds into itself for three flights:
oily eyes look down, receding into the black surfaces of canvas.
Ascent favours the rich and wellborn, posits the rule of day.

But nighttime has hooves, is blushed with the memory
of streaky dawn caped in pigeons' wings: the fresh spill
of unknown rivers runs beneath its grime-furred skin.

Foundling 453, a boy

My Name is Andrews

I have many names: the first my mother gave me –
unfamiliar and spoken elsewhere in sounds far-growing, like footsteps
down a corridor, the reverberant smack of shoe leather on slab

Another is the name I hear every day –
This name mutates by the second:

Jones, Bones, Barnaby Bones,
Barely Barnaby, Barely Bones

Foundling 13287, a boy

Speckled as a quail's egg
and regimental as braid, my cloth
was printed on a bed of nails.

Each twig on *spriged cotten* paths an arc,
red brown and thin as drool, sprouts
exits that stop, go nowhere, belie

growth's root and fervent increase.
These slim stems might have been a map
leading to a rich, exotic

land, or the lines etched on the palm
of my hand, telling of dark
strangers and letters bearing news

Note:
Established in the mid-18th century, the Foundling Hospital in London provided a place
for children whose single mothers could not support them. A mother would leave a token
– usually a square of cloth from the child's clothing – as a means of identifying her child,
should she return.

'*spriged cotten*': how 'sprigged cotton' was spelt on the intake form.

Gemma Green

for John Burnside

Crescent

And if life is a long stick
and I find myself nuzzling it,
feeling out the notches –
I will think again of the necklace of birches
threaded around the crescent,
beaming white in the headlights –
a flash of snow in a dream.

Louise C. Callaghan

The Tapestry Cartoons

His vast oil painted canvases
for the Royal Factory,
known simply as cartoons,
were rolled up one day
and stored away.

Found a century later
in the Summer Palace
at Aranjuez –
what was once discarded,
now on display.

In the Museum of the Prado
you may see
the costumes they wore
and the food they ate
from glazed crockery…

San Isidro's saint-day
on banks of the Manzanares,
a game of blindman's-buff.
A life-size ragdoll,
flung high into the air.

And Goya's extraordinary
feel for detail.
As for the tapestries
for the royal nursery walls,
what has become of them?

Portrait of Sebastián Martínez y Pérez

Emanating calm, he is seated there
on a straight-backed chair
with a dedicatory letter in his hand
that says: *From your friend Goya 1792.*

The artist depicts his sallow skin
as smooth as chamois leather,
and the pomade-powdered wig,
worthy of some local Barber of Seville

in a pearl-grey ribbed jacket,
shadowed like a raincloud.
His canary-yellow breeches are
for all the world *mousseline de soie,*

In this palatial house here in Cádiz
he took care of Goya – recovering
from the illness that left him stone deaf.
Not that they know this yet.

Fransisco de Goya y Lucientes

In *Portrait of the Royal Family* another figure
looks out at the viewer. As Velázquez
portrayed himself at work in *Las Meninas,*
so too Goya presents himself in the picture.
In the penumbra before a sloping canvas
he stands looking over the shoulders
of the thirteen royal family members.
Their gold-embroidered costumes, blue-
and-white-stripe sashes, intricate lace
lend them all the glitz of our *Hola!* generation.
Bourbons, they stare out of small regal eyes
in the sunless chamber. But his find you
in the well-positioned mirror: white-chested,
his pale shadow face. The deafness
already coiled like a trap inside each ear.

William Oxley

Night Fishing at Antibes

(Picasso)

Where have they gone now, the young men
      who were wave-bold?
Carried their boats to the delicious shore
to the nightblue sea to scoop the silver
      of fishscale, the *fruits de mer*,
scrape up from the bed of bubbled silence
langoustine and lobster, oyster and crab?
      Where, where gone? They are old now
and no more young for such precarious
ways. Theirs a dead trade only lives on
      in Pablo's unreasonable colours, netting
of brilliant distortions. Such collisions
in the mind: the luminous configurations
      of very ordinary loss. Alas!
The joyless *joie de vivre* of it all in
blessed Antibes where light and dark thin
      to amazing Provençal purity.
But. But those same twisted figures of dream,
ghouls with razor teeth, and a puerile Neptune
      with a prod-prod trident –
how account for them or the immiscible colours
and the eyes, buttons forever staring?
      Let us say that night fishing
in the moonlit turmoil of the sea, reminds
that life, like truth, is a fishing in darkest
      places, tides and deeps of the mind.

Will Stone

Sometimes This Genius Grows Dark

to Van Gogh

Feeding time in the fields.
Dark riders driving on horses,
flaming cypresses, windmills.
Somehow you must drain it all,
tear through the gauze.
All that's left a single eye that frames,
or this mouth rowing curses
over a lake of wine.
Dawn and a body slumped
in the coffee-threaded pension.
Over a torn brioche you thirst
for the forward dance,
those regiments and chorus lines,
chestnut, beech, sycamore, pine.
The copse calls out only for a moment
and you had to be there
fumbling with the cobalt, the chromium
exhausted by 'unquestioned potential',
the raised canes, the measured admiration.
The one and only arrangement,
a clear shot. Gone . . .
Nature slips behind a cloud.
Nothing remains but your seized prey face
seared by the comet's tail.
Later they gathered for the sonatas.
There you stood behind the player,
her fingers grazing into deep
un-reached black waters.
Insane craving to park your cracked lips
in the inconceivable shelter of her nape.
Now back into the Elysian fields
longing to step off, to strip, to shake trees.
But the sun is devouring your head,
the ruts chuckling at your patched boots.

Blood on the stubble, the rest barrelled
on the iron bed in the tiny room.
You count the canvases they brought,
these carapaces of hope.
They look like friends you once knew,
eight downcast angels bearing their shields.

Ice Warning

Now you feel the ice break away.
Each rooted on his receding floe
and the last hard sellers of hope
slip with seals into dark water.
All are trapped together, even
the blooming girls thirsting
for their first assignments
and painted saints with visible haloes
penned in by faded mortar lines, or
glacial lilies in the Sablon church
sustained by the last ember of their urn.
Wind sifts the chestnuts over a still canal.
From a dark velvet box they lift jewels
and hearts are turned to the past's
always emptying archive of light.
Later on a station concourse,
a homeless man begins to shout,
swings his life on a chain through fetid air
before the exhausted office girls,
descending the iron clad steps,
who do not see and pass on
through the shrivelled leaves
whirling in eddies so furiously,
leaving no trace on the endlessly
swept stairwell.

Andrew McNeillie

Late Spring

I wanted to put elegy into storage
as the album-game de nos jours.
So much loss. Not loss but longing.
I worked on the idea that presence
makes the heart grow fonder
but straightaway found myself here.
It was late spring, the days not yet long
stealing time down cold evenings.
And this to make good
something else I put no name to.

The Big Snow

for Finn McCreath

The old men would speak of it, with warmth,
remembering snow-buntings in the stackyard.
Miracles and snowflakes swarming hard
to hold their ground against wet earth.
How it caught even prudent souls off guard.
And what they meant by big was also lasting.
Men of '47. They could remember wartime news
of Russia as if yesterday; and being themselves still
horse-drawn, praised a shoe would spiel the brae,
of an icy morning, and I was one year old.
Now as old as they, or coming on, to play
their part I speak of rainy summers and
calendars turned inside out, deeper troubles
than ice or snow to guard against, until today.

January 2010

Andrew Waterman

Casualty, 1949

I can't remember, maybe never knew
what I had done to make my gentle Dad
so furious: his flailing round our bedroom
lit on the battleship on the mantelpiece
I'd pasted from a silver-paper kit.
Tears burst from me as he clenched and scrunched it.

He bore no grudge, the next day in the forest,
hands in his trousers-pockets with thumbs jutting
he chipped the ball just right for me to head,
and named more trees and berries and birds singing
than I've known since, or troubled to remember.

At his tool-box he explained to me
the jittery little spirit-level bubble.
A bowl upon the kitchen dresser floated
pungent leaves, 'Your Father's medicine'.

A clearing, sunlit pond where dragonflies
glittered, a hollowed-out tree at its brink
and the cottage where the family were friends.

His suit on the straight-back chair beside his bed,
fragrant with pipe-smoke.
                       Then Mum took me elsewhere.

'Did your Dad die in the War?' I was struck speechless.

The Examination

The signal came somewhere between
sensing the tricks you might work
with an opposable thumb
and mastering fire: *You can look
at the questions and begin.*

*Have a go at them all
within the time allowed
which depends on yourselves.* Some
hung back in caves for a while,
some showed more aptitude
than others, or had better luck:

wigwams and totem poles
didn't quite measure up
to Athens and Angkor Wat;
but problem-solving devices
from the abacus and the axe
to the zeppelin and the zip
brimmed non-stop, cannonballs
smashed castles, Foxton Locks
got boats uphill. You met
with setbacks, suffered falls,
but bounced back from each crisis.

So cities and empires spread,
with many an eye-catching wonder,
the Sphinx, the Blue Mosque, the Louvre,
Big Ben and the Hoover Dam;
you scribbled railways all over
the planet from tropics to tundra;
and your finer thoughts were distilled
by Plato, Li Po, Shakespeare, Freud,
Pascal and Omar Khayyam –
a row of tumblers to hold
the oceans of blood you've shed.

And some of the questions had been
set in invisible ink,

appearing too late, or were born
of your answers: splitting the atom
left you to juggle the Bomb.
Under your talking heads
the space that remains is shrinking,
poisonous with your greeds;
now red alert is blinking,
the virus is in the machine
and all your screens going blank.

Runner

Feet padding up behind me, fast, and coming
abreast he slows, turns to me: twenty-ish,
just thin white shorts and vest against the wintry
sift of rain along the river footpath.
'Which way should I head to reach the airport?'
'At the next bridge go up to the road, turn right,'
I detail junctions, veers, 'then from the Greyhound
keep right on out to the ring-road, cross it,
it's two miles further.'
                                    Rather him than me.
'Thanks.' He scuds off into twilight under
bare trees lurched at the water's edge as if
stunned in mid-spasm, clutching at thin air.

Then it comes back: how once I did all this,
and daily, training, how you bowl along
gulping lungfuls, the world spinning beneath
your feet, the streetlamps flicking overhead,
reeling in distance, home with all that time
for evenings deep in books, or seeing friends.

How has time got so much less? Why have I never,
and now never shall, become...
                                    But it's not those
far-flung goals all around ambition's compass
that ail me, but things missed out near-at-hand.

Leaves lie shoaled, and as I've not since childhood
I stoop, scoop up an armful, glistening, rustling,
then shudder with the pang of realising
I cannot name the trees above them. Rain
fresh as ever on my cheeks, my hands
let their freight splash gently back to earth
they've rarely dug, and never made a garden.

Quick as a Flash

Playground zoomings, muddied knees,
frogspawn, cycling with no brakes,
scrumping, skimming stones on lakes,
dangling upside-down in trees;

balanced eager at the top
of the helter-skelter you
launched yourself to whoosh down through
promised thrills and spills non-stop.

No-one warned you, if they did
you weren't listening. Though it may
all still seem only yesterday
you're older now than Uncle Sid

doddering about back then.
Now foretellings, evidence
of things to come smite every sense
and swirl like snow. Here again

where you sit, at intervals
bobbing out of little rooms
file in hand, a doctor comes
peering left and right, and calls

a name: 'Anne Pretty!' 'Albert Gore!'
'Iris Speed!' 'Hugh Hope!' 'Jean Quick!' –
who's next to you. She grips her stick
and makes it wheezing to his door.

Some look absolutely crocked,
need arms or wheeling, fall asleep,
somehow get done, but more such keep
filtering in, all cruelly mocked

by mags laid out to be leafed through
stuffed with features on the young
and fit and beautiful, among
whom once… But now the call's for you…

The check finds nothing sinister
this time. You book the next, and get
out fast (your legs aren't rhubarb yet),
and gratefully gulp in fresh air.

Aviva Dautch

Grasshoppers

for John Burnside

We were in our own sight like grasshoppers, and so we were in their sight.

Numbers 13:33

It's all about perspective, how we view ourselves.
Light falls on water at an angle:
midday and the art-deco panes
refract sun onto the bath
until meniscus becomes mirror
and the curve of your knee describes
a complete arc.   You jam your feet
flat against the side of the tub and
 the surface of water intersects
      with joints, making toes
simultaneously above and below the line:
   an imperfect reflection wavering with each movement
      so you strain to be still
and stillness means silence.
     All there is: the body's hollows,
its valleys and folds, landscape of fleshy murmurs,
     and your intruding heartbeat
insistent as a locust
snapping its wings in flight.

*

Rustle of paper – flicking pages –
      Chekhov's *The Grasshopper*, perhaps?
You read yourself as Olga Ivanova
    on a moonlit night in July,
standing riverside with Rybakovsky who
sweet-talks you away from your husband
     with whispers of shadows and mortality,
who has a thousand reasons for crying yet sheds no tears.
Your lover is mercurial, crushing –

beside him you feel shame,
  are not an artist but an insect,
    small, unfaithful,
dreaming of rain
        on the Volga.

       *

Why do you let time drift
    until the water is tepid
and you're all wrinkles and flexion?

       *

According to Aesop
    Grasshopper has no fear, no forethought.
He whiles away the summer playing
as Ant works hard.
  Winter comes and Grasshopper
begs for shelter but Ant leaves
  him starving, exposed.
      Death by improvidence –
most human of weaknesses.

       *

Your mind hops between
    the cruelty of the ant
and the cruelty of Olga,
neglecting her doctor husband,
        forsaking vows for art.

       *

Toes are a miracle of articulation,
providing us with balance and thrust.
    You turn their weight-bearing
into metaphor: where the whole individuates
    it can carry the rest;
what comes to mind is 'community'.

The Rabbis define community
    as 'ten'.   Twelve spies sent
to scout out Canaan, flowing with milk and honey,

with grapes and olives, pomegranates and figs.
          Only two return with a positive view,
the rest too scared to enter their (already occupied)
promised land.   Ten –
          a community who challenged their leader
and mistrusted God. In their own eyes
   they were frail creatures:
          grasshoppers among giants.

                    *

The moment of disconnect occurs when you
float out of your body
          and see from above:
flesh as canvas, as fields and fruit,
as biblical abundance, *nature-mort*.

                    *

Your American friend tells you that this year in Nebraska
the bugs are swarming. They'll chomp down
on anything, flowing over roads, fields,
fences, barns, hanging laundry, plagues
of mormon crickets, of cannibalistic katydids,
          feasting on grain until nothing is left.

You imagine the colony
          blanketing the earth:
a host of single organisms.

A grasshopper's sense organs consist
of tiny fibres – sensilla – calibrated
          to respond to external stimuli.

You are covered in goosebumps, each blonde hair
crawling from root to tip,
                    moving individually but as one.

                    *

The sound of gunfire!
          Is it rain ricocheting off
                    the attic roof
or the shower
          strafing your skin?

*

Territory is considered occupied
    when it is actually placed under the authority of the hostile army.
The occupation extends
        only to the territory where such authority
                has been established and can be exercised.

The authority of the legitimate power
        having in fact passed into the hands of the occupant,
the latter shall take all the measures   *in his power*
  to restore,
        and ensure,
            as far as possible,
public order and safety,
    while respecting, unless absolutely prevented, the laws in force in the country.

*

Within and without are one –
there is no exterior view, or perhaps it's a double exposure,
        when you stare from windows
at night into the room's interior
        superimposed onto the dark street.

Is all this introspection avoidance? A way
        not to look out?

You are terrified of your own infidelity,
        the lover's betrayal.

And so you occupy your mind with tangents
        and nightmares,
with theology and art.

And so you lose yourself in water until boundaries are blurred,
        until there are no boundaries.

And so the body becomes your territory:
        a land where the grasshoppers swarm.

Note:
The penultimate section of this poem quotes Articles 42 & 43 of the *Hague Conventions*
(1907): 'Section III Military Authority over the territory of the hostile State'.

87

Lynn Roberts

Lunchtime with Eros

Run your fingernail along my arm once more,
so the down shivers erect like grass plumes
and brushes – kisses – against your own; your
warmth breathes out over my skin and heat blooms,
smoothing it there – just there; and all the while
our arms lie quietly on the table top,
not touching, and our eyes don't meet. Your smile
is printed for me on your glass, the knop
stamped with your fingerprints, and on your plate
crumbs and a cheap old nickel fork contain
your DNA – spirals of life which wait
like flies in amber, microscopic chain
of polymers – codes which infiltrate
this bar, transfiguring the mundane.

Melinda Lovell

Making a Five Element Love Poem

Seeing his wife as his earth
Neruda sprinkles her lavishly, with sonnets.
She is cousin to oregano,
she brings him metaphors, in dozens

But I, who am your woman, your scent
(one who grows herbs around and between)
I say you, the man, who cooks, are
my earth, and cousin to hawthorn
(whose berries make it glow with fire)
you cook from its heart's sureness

In your scrubbing, chopping, pounding
is the turning-to-good
of root, bruised green, seed, blood

Inside your humming heart I smile at
a cove of sea salt, noble onion tears,
heather honey with its steadfast gleam

At your heart's outer leaf, I overhear
sweetness of certain pears conversing
with crisp bitterness of chicory – such gossip –

I hear lightness of wine corks popping

I, the woman, would become scentless
without these spells of yours –
pan on flame, spitting oil,
rueful wisdom of vinegar

Note:
In traditional Five Element Chinese Medicine, the five elements have five corresponding
tastes: sour, bitter, sweet, pungent, salty

David Borthwick

'To Comfort me with Nothing':
John Burnside's Dissident Poetics

John Burnside has defined his poetic task in terms of dissidence. Not, he admits, political dissidence of the more common sort, but understood in its seventeenth-century sense as 'a forme of prayer dissident from the common.' For Burnside, this form of dissidence manifests itself in our own time as:

> a refusal to use the prescribed words, a refusal to pray to the false gods; a refusal to serve the apparatus of commercial and cultural imperialism that gives us GM crops, collectible *Lord of the Rings* memorabilia and Reality TV. A refusal to be party to the universal lie.[1]

Since the publication in 1988 of his debut collection *The Hoop*, Burnside's poetic output has been prolific. From the outset, though, his work has shown a remarkable dedication to a tightly focused range of themes. Burnside's verse is, as James McGonigal has noted, 'attuned to a radical hunger for alternatives to … politicised transnational capitalism, and the reticence or caution of traditional religious structures in response to it.'[2] While Burnside's poetic output may seem in this sense to appeal to a contemporary *zeitgeist*, I would argue that his particular response comes in the form of an earth-centred poetics and a commitment to spiritual contemplation of humanity's plight in the face of environmental degradation. 'What matters now,' Burnside claims, 'is the poetry of "we": preserving the environment and studying how we human beings should dwell on the earth without destroying it.'[3] Fairly recently, the term ecopoetry has emerged as the preferred term of poets and critics to describe poetry that responds to environmental crisis. Introducing his anthology *Earth Shattering: Ecopoems* (2007), Neil Astley describes some of the features associated with ecopoetry:

---

[1] John Burnside, *A Poet's Polemic: Poetry, Dissidence and Reality TV* (Strangefruit/National Poetry Day, 2003), pp. 4–5.

[2] 'Translating God: Negative Theology and Two Scottish Poets,' *Ethically Speaking: Voice and Values in Modern Scottish Writing*, ed. by James McGonigal and Kirsten Stirling (Amsterdam, Rodopi, 2006), pp. 223–49 (p. 235).

[3] Attila Dósa, 'An Interview with John Burnside,' *Scottish Studies Review*, 4.1 (Spring 2003), pp. 9–24 (p. 11).

ecopoetry goes beyond traditional nature poetry to take on distinctly contemporary issues [...] Ecopoems dramatise the dangers and poverty of a modern world perilously cut off from nature and ruled by technology, self-interest and economic power. [4]

More than this, ecopoetry refers to verse rooted in a distinct mindset; it describes a mode of metaphysical enquiry which recognises our profound alienation from the natural world and suggests ways of enacting a reconnection, however tentative that may be.

Throughout his poetic output so far Burnside has employed Christian imagery to account for the ways in which contemplation of, and immersion in, the natural world can result in profound emotional and spiritual connections which address the distance between the individual and what is, after all, our original habitat. In his collection *The Myth of the Twin* (1994), 'angels arrive through the hedge' ('Angels Eyes') while washing dried outdoors has 'the smell of a resurrection' ('R.E.'); meanwhile, another speaker perceives 'a faint god's partial emergence / through willow and alder' ('The Solitary in Autumn'). For all this, Burnside's use of Christian imagery is hardly conventional. His collection *The Good Neighbour* (2005) includes a series of poems titled after, and which deal with, forms of annunciation, which he describes in terms of 'something divine confronting the soul.' These lyrics are characterised by a powerful sense of the numinous or emergent which arrives, according to Burnside, 'when we're quiet enough for the question to be asked of us.' He continues: 'in a sense the poems are a kind of inverse prayer.'[5] These are poems borne of spiritual contemplation and pervigilation rather than divine intervention; they are lyrics which document 'the creak and whisper of the night's / improbable apparatus, lacewings and frost / and starlight on the rooftops like a veil' ('Annunciation with Zero Point Field'). Particularly Catholic imagery persists throughout Burnside's verse, but it is simultaneously endorsed and denied, partially emptied of its traditional applications and connotations. In *Swimming in the Flood* (1995), his lyric sequence 'Parousia' – the second coming – recalls a childhood fear of meeting Christ in the edgelands of 'timber yards' and 'oil drums full of rain': 'the silver of fish blood and bone / in the whites of his eyes.' In this sequence the child conflates images taken from Christian teachings with his

---

[4] Neil Astley, ed., *Earth Shattering: Ecopoems* (Tarset: Bloodaxe, 2007), p. 15.
[5] John Burnside, 'on Three Annunciation Poems': *New Writing 13*: Themes, British Council Website (2006), accessed at http://newwriting.britishcouncil.org/all/themes/?theme=18, 17 April 2009.

own experience of nature's mystery, leading to a hybrid understanding of spiritual and natural resurrection: 'the hard bud splitting through ice / and the nailed palm healing.' In Burnside's verse, Christian imagery is used to suggest investment in a patient attention and contemplation which is rewarded with small moments of partial epiphany. 'De corporis resurrectione', collected in *Gift Songs* (2007), contains the lines:

> I still imagine a return,
> though never quite the god they talked about
>
> in Sunday school: more atmosphere than flesh,
> this almost taking form as frequency,
> like static, or the fuzz of radio.

Here, we have 'atmosphere' rather than flesh, an 'almost' taking form, an immanent presence that is *like* static *or* the fuzz of radio. This is an emergence that is 'never quite,' where all descriptions fail. Immanence is gestured at through forms of domestic electricity, slight and surprising, comforting even, rather than revelatory or imbued with prophetic significance.

In many of his poems, one of Burnside's preferred lexical choices is 'something.' To take two such examples from *The Light Trap* (2002): 'one bright afternoon, / in wintertime, // something will come from nowhere / and touch a man' ('After Lucretius'); or 'something was always present in the snow / that fell between our parish and the next' ('Being and Time'). These 'somethings' are never fully defined in Burnside's verse; they remain open, tentative, self-consciously bereft of a noun that would impose final meaning. The word is used to suggest liminal states and emergent presences, those experiences which 'slip through the network of classifications that normally locate states and positions in cultural space.'[6] 'Something' is used to suggest a spiritual presence that exists between boundaries, summoning at once mystery and emptiness. This is a feature of Burnside's verse that critics have found unsatisfying. John Lucas, for example, is particularly perplexed: 'the numinous can't, I realise, be seized as you'd grip a piece of coal with tongs, but there are moments in this poet's work when, for all its accomplishment, it is resolute only in its irresolution.'[7] Graeme Richardson is less charitable,

---

[6] Victor W. Turner, *The Ritual Process: Structure and Anti-Structure* (London: Routledge and Kegan Paul, 1969), p. 95.
[7] John Lucas, 'Souls, Ghosts, Angels and "Things Not Human": John Burnside, Alice Oswald and Kathleen Jamie', *PN Review*, 177 (2007), pp. 27–32 (p. 29).

referring to Burnside's exploration of the numinous as 'sentimentalised unknowing.' [8]

It is certainly hard to know how to account for Burnside's employment of Christian imagery, particularly since he has been so vocal in his rejection of religious belief, claiming to endorse agnosticism because, he argues, 'there can be no rational proof of god's presence or absence.' He continues further: 'the whole god question is the basis for a deliberate, mostly fearful limitation of the possibilities that the world offers.'[9] One the one hand, Burnside endorses rationality, the need for empirical proof; on the other, insists upon freedom from a single system of interpretation or belief: scientific certainty *and* a sense of the numinous or emergent.

It is this apparently paradoxical fusion that Burnside deals with in a number of his poems, which scrupulously employ taxonomic descriptions of animal and plant life, yet insist that the sum of the parts is greater than mere categorisation can acknowledge or account for. In 'Taxonomy,' the speaker notes:

> though we mostly look for what we know,
> there is something we love in ourselves
>
> that a meadow answers:
> the blue of an upland flower
> or a tideline of grass;
>
> the heart-shaped
> or spatulate leaf
> of toadflax, or fern.

He concludes by dwelling on:

> the given and the named
> discovered and invented
> one more time,
>
> with each new bud or tendril that unfolds
> upon the revelation
> of the known
> > (*The Light Trap*, 2002).

---

[8] Graeme Richardson, 'John Burnside's Poetry: No Ideas but in Somethings,' *Areté* 10 (Winter 2002), accessed at www.aretemagazine.com, 7 November 2008.

[9] John Burnside, review of Michel Onfray, *In Defence of Atheism*, *Scotsman*, 3 June 2007.

In 'De Anima,' another speaker encounters a bird he has no name for, 'a migrant foreigner that must have strayed,' whose song is 'so much a question to the self I was / I came through / on the far side of the day / uncertain / plundered / given up for lost' (*The Good Neighbour*, 2005). In Burnside's poetry, his speakers are forever ready to be 'given up for lost,' to accept that the known world, defined and understood as system, as ecology even, is insufficient to account for one's experience of truly dwelling on the earth as a spiritual being attempting to find meaning, and a means to engage with nature.

Since his collection *The Asylum Dance* (2000), Burnside's verse has been influenced by ideas originating in the philosophy of Martin Heidegger. Heidegger's work has recently experienced a resurgence, thanks in part to its relevance to an emerging scholarly field known as ecocriticism. Ecocritics take an interdisciplinary approach to literary study, examining texts in the context of evolving ideas about the natural world over time and also considering how literature can inform and document environmental ideas. Many of these critics argue that it is a sense of alienation from nature, of homelessness and exile, experienced by largely urban human populations (particularly in the West), which licences the destruction of nature. The natural world is seen as purely a resource for human use, thus aiding and abetting environmental crisis. One of Heidegger's most relevant concepts here is that of 'dwelling' and it is this notion in particular that we can see deployed and negotiated with in Burnside's work. 'Dwelling' has been defined as a studied and continuous process, 'learning to find a place on the earth which does not dominate, manipulate, pollute or destroy it.'[10] More than this, 'dwelling' entails an acceptance and exploration of rootedness in place and time, as Greg Garrard explains: '"Dwelling" is not a transient state; rather, it implies the long-term imbrication of humans in a landscape of memory, ancestry and death, of ritual, life and work.'[11] To 'dwell,' then, is not merely to find a conservationist response to habitat, it is also to view oneself as part of a narrative of 'dwelling' in a particular place; it is to effect a sustained continuance in harmony with, rather than in opposition to, the natural and non-human world. This ascetic, for that is what it is, manifests itself in Burnside's work in a number of complimentary ways. In particular, Heidegger's concept of 'the fourfold' is instructive. Heidegger says:

---

[10] Laurence Coupe, introduction to 'Earth, Memory and Critique of Modernity,' in *The Green Studies Reader: From Romanticism to Ecocriticism*, ed. Laurence Coupe (London: Routledge, 2000), pp. 61–5 (p. 64).

[11] Greg Garrard, *Ecocriticism* (London: Routledge, 2004), p. 109.

human being consists in dwelling and, indeed, dwelling in the sense of the stay of mortals on the earth.

But 'on the earth' already means 'under the sky.' Both of these *also* mean 'remaining before the divinities' and include a 'belonging to men's being with one another. By a *primal* oneness the four – earth and sky, divinities and mortals – belong together in one.[12]

Heidegger's 'fourfold' requires a profound openness to and acceptance of the essential nature of the earth's elements, including humanity. He demands a personal discipline committed to respecting the intrinsic qualities of nature rather than considering its features solely in terms of instrumental use: 'Mortals dwell in that they receive the sky as sky. They leave to the sun and moon their journey, to the stars their courses, to the seasons their blessing and their inclemency' (Heidegger, p. 150). This ecology of the fourfold – earth, sky, divinities and mortals – does not deny scientific knowledge or taxonomic categorisation of natural elements, but, interpreted for a contemporary world, it also insists upon a spiritual dimension which inhabits the space between taxonomy and the world, refusing the finalisation, or limitation, which definition from a purely anthropocentric discipline may imply. Between the elements of 'the fourfold' there is the possibility for the spiritual, that which cannot be systematised, a perhaps purely personal, but no less authentic, engagement with the natural and non-human world. Rather than enacting a 'sentimentalised unknowing' in his verse, then, I would contend that Burnside is perfectly conscious of his tendency towards irresolution; furthermore, I would argue that he seeks to evade any concrete finalisation of the constituents by which he documents his speakers' encounters and beliefs. Rather, he purposefully avoids limitation and definition.

Indeed, alongside his more Christian imagery, we find frequently in Burnside's verse natural phenomena juxtaposed with elements suggestive of pagan symbolism. In 'Lapsed,' the speaker talks of childhood visions of 'Christ / in the afternoon sun' but goes on: 'that presence dissolved, / I cling to the relics I find in water and loam' (*The Myth of the Twin*, 1994). In 'Animism' the speaker tells an unidentified addressee: 'you always verged upon / the older forms of prayer, / unveiling bees and starlings in the roof, lacewings and frogs' (*The Light Trap*, 2002). The final poem in *Gift Songs* (2007) speaks alike of 'meeting with the god, that stink of goat' but also: 'hairless angels stepping from the rain.' In his verse, Burnside constructs a

---

[12] Martin Heidegger, *Poetry, Language, Thought*, trans. Albert Hofstadter (New York: Harper and Row, 1971), p. 149.

very 'personal reliquary' (Lucas, p. 28), a fusion of reflections both Catholic and pagan, in an attempt to explore what it means to contemplate, and immerse oneself in, the non-human world. I would describe Burnside as a '*bricoleur*,' a term first employed by anthropologist Claude Levi-Strauss in his *The Savage Mind* (1962) and adapted from the activities of the French *bricoleur*, or handyman, someone who makes use of the various materials which come to hand, who performs an eclectic form of craftsmanship. In bringing together Christian and pagan images to describe and accentuate unclassifiable states of being, Burnside's technique may be described as a form of mytho-spirtual *bricolage*.

Burnside's poetry to date employs this technique allied to observance of a calendar rooted in a culture of feast days, Christian and pagan, which respond to the cycles of nature. Prominent among these is the festival of Hallowe'en (the old Celtic new year, according to some sources) but also the season of, as James McGonigal has noted, 'what Catholics call "the communion of the saints" (a deep sense of the spiritual unity of the living and the dead, and of the loving duty of the living to pray for the dead...).'[13] Burnside's poetic 'dwelling' calls for the inclusion of those who have passed, who provide a narrative of continuity of human habitation and activity: 'the dead we have washed and buried: / the sweet-mouthed, arthritic mothers we rarely noticed / polishing spoons in the small hours / polishing mirrors.' These are 'the dead we have numbered and set aside' who 'will blossom again in ditch-moss and columns of ivy // replacing themselves in the lull of the visible world / with fingerprints; voices, blood blisters; rose tattoos' ('De Corporis Resurrectione', *Gift Songs*). The winter and spring festivals Burnside summons are not only a means of drawing together human cultural cycles with those of the natural world, but also of emphasising the continuity that each cycle shares with the other, our rootedness in that cycle, nature and culture as one persisting entity, which humanity can only acknowledge in ceremony, myth and symbol.

Of course, there has long existed the problematic of culture-nature dualism in Western epistemology and this is perhaps the principal reason that we cannot find a means to connect directly with the non-human world. As Jonathan Bate has, somewhat pessimistically, stated: 'locked in the prison-house of language, dwelling in the *logos* not the *oikos*, we know only the text, not the land'[14]. Bate also contends, however, that poetry can nevertheless provide 'not a description of dwelling with the earth, not a disengaged

---

[13] James McGonigal, 'Millennial Days: Religion as Consolation and Desolation in Contemporary Scottish Poetry,' *Revista Canaria de Estudios Ingleses*, 41 (2000), pp. 55–76 (p. 59).
[14] Jonathan Bate, *The Song of the Earth* (London: Picador, 2001), p. 237.

thinking about it, but an *experiencing* of it' (Bate, p. 42, my emphasis). I think this lies at the crux of what John Burnside is trying to achieve. He employs metaphor, symbol and myth to present finely nuanced poems whose aesthetic and emotional effects are designed to replicate the experience of connection between the human and non-human worlds. These poems emphasise our own connection to and rootedness in natural history. Robert Pogue Harrison has pointed out that 'the Greek word *logos* is usually translated as "language", but more originally it means "relation". *Logos* is that which binds, gathers, or relates.'[15] Using an eclectic range of references to cultural practices and exact natural-historical descriptions of plants and animals, Burnside attempts to gather or relate these to suggest a mode of 'dwelling.' His technique is perhaps best summed up by poet Tim Lilburn:

> contemplation grows out of the wreckage of other forms of knowing .... Language breaks up in it, identity breaks up, consolation is disassembled ... the desire to know the world behind its names is the death of knowing which is objective, ordering, communicable and the apparently secure life that rests on such knowing.[16]

In a secular, urban-based and even virtual world, Burnside can only communicate essential connections to the earth through the wreckage of previous systems of knowing. However, this allows a freedom from system and order which, while disruptive of certainty or closure, allows him to chart a different means of 'dwelling.' This is achieved formally as well as thematically. 'Ny-Hellesund,' for example, contains the following passage:

> the corn is full of skylarks;
> the last of the daylight
> simmers above the wood
> where chiffchaff and warblers
> parley from shade to shade,
> becoming the air
> in a song that exists for nothing.

---

[15] Robert Pogue Harrison, *Forests: The Shadow of Civilisation* (London: University of Chicago Press, 1992), p. 200.

[16] Tim Lilburn, 'How To Be Here?' *Poetry and Knowing: Speculative Essays and Interviews*, ed. Tim Lilburn (Kingston, Ontario: Quarry Press, 1995), pp. 161–76 (p. 168).

Everything maps its world
and what world there is
is the current sum
of all our navigation:
networks of panic and longing,
road maps in gorse,
the river at twilight
vanishing into the sway
of cattle and bees
                    (*Gift Songs*, 2007).

This fragment is made resonant by a particular technique pointed out perceptively by John Lucas, who describes how Burnside creates:

a kind of paratactic fusion so that, by implication or by what we may infer, everything is potentially linked to everything else, and a world we are accustomed to experiencing as collocations of disparate fragments can be set against and ... displaced by one of coherence
                    (Lucas, p. 29).

Indeed, the passage from 'Ny-Hellesund' is made up of largely unrelated phrases which, through form – visual and occasionally semantic ('networks' and 'roadmaps,' for example) – suggest, by accretion, some kind of ecological unity. This poetic technique mimics in language a connection to the ecosystem that human abilities, sensory and cerebral, do not on the whole permit, as Karl Kroeber has noted:

the unity of an ecosystem ... is not something sensorily perceptible, even though it is determinative of our sensory experience. Nor is the entirety of the system readily definable in traditionally logical terms, even though reason is essential to our understanding of it.[17]

What Burnside attempts to provide, then, is a simulation of, a poetic response to – or, in Bate's words, an *experiencing of* – an ecological unity in which self and other, the human in contemplation and the landscape he is immersed in, form an interrelated totality, a site of 'dwelling.' This is a state rendered poetically, of course, in an imaginative space which, as Kroeber

---

[17] Karl Kroeber, *Ecological Literary Criticism: Romantic Imagining and the Biology of Mind* (New York: Columbia University Press, 1994), p. 58.

intimates, 'tends not to lead toward what we think of as a *realpolitik.*' Yet Burnside's project has never been dissident in this sense. Perhaps his work may be qualified using McGonigal's term for Burnside's work: recusant, refusing to submit to the authority of any single theological or mythical ordering perspective.[18] Rather, his poems use forms of language, myth and symbol which many would consider to be contingent, only for Burnside to reveal through these a wholly necessary connection to nature. The connection is a vital one, but by definition it cannot fully satisfy, since it offers no afterlife but memory, and no resolution but in continuance, existing as something like:

a murmur that comes through the wind,
a hand's-breadth, a wingspan,

arriving from nowhere, or conjured out of the dark
between the near field and the kitchen door,
to sound me out, to comfort me with nothing
('By Pittenweem', *Gift Songs*, 2007).

---

[18] James McGonigal, 'Recusant Grace: The Religious Impulse in John Burnside's Verse,' *Verse*, vol. 10, no. 1 (Spring 1993), pp. 65–72.

Andy Brown

Finding 'The Lit Space': Reality, Imagination, and the Commonplace, in the Poetry of John Burnside

This essay examines John Burnside's idea of 'the lit space' – a dwelling space which originates in the commonplace, and acts as a crucible for fusing reality and imagination into lyric ecopoetry, asking questions of us about how we ourselves should dwell.

Burnside's poems are grounded in organic formation, authenticity, and a rejection of self-conscious artfulness. He composes in the head and, citing Mandelstam, acknowledges that 'the real thing happens [...] on the lips' (Dosa 22). Poetry for Burnside is an act of healing through utterance: 'What I'm writing is always about healing: about healing the world or about trying to heal one's vision of the world' (22). His collection *Swimming in the Flood* even concludes with the word 'healing', after presenting some poetic sequences that explore 'the inexplicable malice of being' (23). Burnside's novels, also famously dark, often explore forms of violence and yet Burnside reminds us that 'Violence is a symptom of a spiritual failure, a failure to recognise the fundamental imperative to respect and honour "the other"' (19). One great violence is that perpetrated against the world in which we dwell.

For Burnside, this 'dwelling' is therefore a spiritual act, as much as a political and poetic one, a distinction that helps distance him perhaps from 'nature poetry' and aligns him with current trends in ecopoetics, as critic Jonathan Bate says, poetry that 'presents the experience of dwelling' (42), in a philosophical yet non-didactic way. Burnside's ecopoetics and politics contrast to his early career in computer programming, in that they are firmly grounded in the commonplace and the real: 'I feel that I've had far too much interest in the virtual, and I'm interested in the *real*' (Dosa 17). In his own essay 'Poetry as Ecology', Burnside makes repeated references to the 'spectacle' and 'beauty' of *the real*: 'Though sometimes we are embarrassed to say it, what we need to say, what we need to remember above and beyond all our other concerns is that this is the real world, this is our enduring mystery' (in Robert Crawford 91). 'Poetry as Ecology' envisions poetry as 'a technique for reclaiming the authentic, a method for reinstating the real, a politics of the actual' (in Crawford 95). It is through the real that we come to the wonderment of the present moment, he argues, 'the way things are real: a blackbird, a scribble of thorns, / a quickening into the moment, the present tense' (*Myth of the Twin* 53).

These issues are central to Burnside's second collection, *Common*

Knowledge, with its epigram from Marx: 'It is common knowledge that the forest echoes back what you shout into it.' The forest clearly places us in the territory of myth (as well as in the wild), representing something primitive within ourselves; a place to which we are both drawn and, simultaneously, of which we are afraid. It is, as Burnside describes in his poem 'Sea Slug'

> Something you might never want to surface –
> though you contain it
> silently within you like a last
> vestige of the naked
> (*Common* 57).

The forest also stands in relation to the social; the person shouting into the forest is, implicitly, at the edge of the forest; at the edge of civilized culture. *Common Knowledge* is then, unsurprisingly, a collection abundant in boundaries and thresholds – suburbs, windows, the surfaces of ponds, gates, fences, and graveyards.[1] As in much folklore, what is (un)known lies at the edge of the self, at the edge of community, rubbing shoulders with our other selves; our possible selves; those other beings that represent who, or what, we might have been, or might want to become. In the poem 'Bethany', this knowledge is the stuff of 'normal life', although made mysterious in how it echoes back to us from the 'forest' of our shared unconscious:

> Normal life: but somewhere in the house
> hidden in the jars and folded string,
> the sudden other – who you meant to be –
> running like a game of Chinese Whispers
> (*Common* 55).

This shared *otherness,* is developed in the poem 'Language', whereby language is *othered* one step further:

> The deep house; the other.
> Names I have yet to find
> on the borders of language,
> words between *silt* and *swan*
> denoting the fishpool and the tree fern

---

[1] As the phenomenologist Gaston Bachelard tells us, and as Burnside is only too aware, 'The poet speaks on the threshold of being' (Bachelard *xvi*).

household that stands for the self
in dreams: the mysterious,
perched on the tripwire of being
another's exact opposition
(*Common* 33).

Burnside urges us to respect this otherness (vis-à-vis his comments on
violence), whether it be found in nature, in others, or in language, precisely
because it stems from our common humanity: 'The kind of poetry I write
is a constant search for the authentic, but not outside the common, lived
experience. It's the commonplace that is real' (Dosa 14). And the commonplace
is located, of course, in the everyday.

Illuminations of the everyday abound in Burnside's work, as in:

Late afternoon in October:
light feathers the kitchen walls,
finds long-lost cousins
in saucepans and colanders
(*Common* 62)

and the prose poem sequences 'Annunciations' and 'Suburbs' in which we
read of the 'kinship of everyday objects [...] surfacing, now and always, into
the moment' (*Common* 47); the word 'surfacing' implying a rise from the
depths of their own *othered* (and perhaps only fleetingly knowable) being, as
well as a rise from the depths ('The deep house') of language.

This binary of self and other, individual and commonality, forms the
central concern of *Common Knowledge*: the self is not something contained
only within ourselves; it is social, and often wild, constantly transgressing
boundaries and borders; slipping through the gaps between them. Our
individual rituals and the social meanings that accrue to them through
repetition (including our use of language), take on symbolic roles in his
poetry. There is a non-religious spirituality at work here – one that strives for
transcendence through the transformation of quotidian things – and which
'rescues mystery from the commonplace', to build that sense of wonderment
with which Burnside's readers are so familiar.

Burnside's sixth collection, *A Normal Skin*, develops the idea of home so
central to all his collections. It was the first book published after his return to
living in Scotland, and the first published after his marriage. That togetherness
here finds intimate expression in the exquisite sequence 'Epithalamium', as
well as the many addresses to a domestic 'you' or 'she':

> She knows how things are made – that's not the point –
> What matters is the order she creates
> And fixes in her mind:
> A map of cogs and springs, laid out in rows,
> Invisibly numbered.
> What we desire in pain
> Is order, the impression of a life
> That cannot be destroyed, only dismantled
> (*Asylum* 1).

Burnside develops his poem with musical variation: 'What we desire in pain / is reason', reason here being metonymic for the previously stated 'order', and that 'order' being something that can be 'fixed in the mind', in the imagination.

The imagination is further signalled in 'Children Sledding in the Dark, Magdalen Green', where the children 'hold the glow / of the imagined' (*Asylum* 36); or in 'Shiochie's Hill, Dunkeld', in which the narrator speaks of attaining the 'hill of the fairies' as a way of getting back to the 'old form of knowledge', even though the poet recognises that whilst 'I could say they are only / imagined, / the shiver that puts them there is real' (*Asylum* 37). *Nota bene*, a bodily shiver, not a mental faculty; not a thought, but something physical: 'a wish for something quick against the skin' (37). Explicit reference to imagination as an intuitive faculty with which we perceive the world, comes in lines such as 'You carry home the snake you thought / was sunning itself on a rock / at the river's edge' ('Snake', *Asylum* 5), where the emphasis of the line break at 'thought', magically turns the snake into an imagined one. Yes, the snake is, of course, *in a poem*, but we believe that it is a real snake in an imaginary garden (echoing Marianne Moore's celebrated 'Poetry', 1935, in which she demands of poetry that it perform the magical trick of presenting 'imaginary gardens with real toads in them'). Burnside's image is developed further as the woman seems to *become* the snake herself by the poem's end, in which she 'shuffles off' the womanliness he has always assumed to be a part of her self, in much the same way as the snake sloughs off its skin.

Such animistic transformations are commonplace in Burnside. In 'Scavenger', the narrator admits 'all the time I long for transformation' (*Normal* 9), whilst in a later poem, 'Kestrel', we read of how 'each body wills its transformation' (*Asylum* 64). The 'I' becomes fused with 'the badger in the soul, the totem beast' mentioned in the poem 'Ghost', or with the deer in the final poem of *A Normal Skin*, 'Penitence'. In this poem, a deer is knocked over by the narrator's car and, after a few moments, slips off into the darkness, alive and well, or injured and about to die, no one knows for sure. When the narrator returns to the site of the crash on subsequent occasions, the deer has somehow become one with the narrator who must return, penitentially, for the damage he may have caused: 'my own flesh in the body of the deer' (61). It is in such transformations – the real-world animal, fused with the internal world of human imagination and spirit – that we recognise Burnside's characteristic metaphysics. Time and again, the narrators of his poems seem to be 'listening; / if anything exists besides ourselves', acknowledging that if there is, 'I'll hear it on the air' ('Scavenger' 8). This idea echoes Wallace Stevens in 'Not Ideas about the Thing but the Thing Itself', his last published poem.[2] Burnside has also written a sonnet-like poem of the same title:

> I was standing out in the field,
> in the first snowfall of winter,
> watching the moon scud clouds
> like a fat carp drifting through water.
> Something had gone before me to the cold
> centre of the wood
> and I walked after, following a trail
> of pawprints that rose through the grass
> a step at a time, till it seemed
> I was stalking myself towards
> some animal brightness hidden in the snow:
> a tension; the casual mention in a song
> of fox; a given, unrepentant life;
> the knowledge of an old reality
> > (*Feast Days* 43),

whilst Wallace Stevens' poem reads:

> At the earliest ending of winter,
> In March, a scrawny cry from outside
> Seemed like a sound in his mind.
>
> He knew that he heard it,
> A bird's cry, at daylight or before,
> In the early March wind.

---

[2] There are other small homages to Stevens in Burnside's poetry, not least the harbinger blackbird in '*Muerte A Lo Lejos*' ('Death in the Distance') in *Feast Days*; a symbolic figure who flies straight out of Stevens' 'Thirteen Ways…' and who comes back to haunt the pages of Burnside's eighth collection, *The Light Trap* in numerous ways. Stephens' words are also present as epigrams to *A Normal Skin* and in Burnside's fourth collection, *The Myth of the Twin*, in the poem 'Variation on a Theme of Wallace Stevens'.

The sun was rising at six,
No longer a battered panache above snow…
It would have been outside.

It was not from the vast ventriloquism
Of sleep's faded papier-mâché…
The sun was coming from outside.

That scrawny cry – it was
A chorister whose c preceded the choir.
It was part of the colossal sun,

Surrounded by its choral rings,
Still far away. It was like
A new knowledge of reality   (466).

The poems have different settings, although they share a broad season. Burnside's poem is set 'in the first snowfall of winter', whilst Stevens' poem is 'At the earliest ending of Winter / In March'. Stevens writes of a bird's cry; 'a scrawny cry from outside', whilst Burnside echoes this in 'the casual mention in a song / of fox'. In the original poem, Stevens also alludes to song, although the 'scrawny cry' becomes fused with the choral song of the sun. Burnside features the moon; Stevens, the sun. Both poets feature the snow, although Stevens' snow is melting in the new warmth, whilst Burnside's is falling, the cold beginning to set in. Both poets feature an observing/hearing 'I', drawn into the depths of the world outside by something animal; the stalked animal in Burnside's poem characteristically becoming the self; the animal in Stevens' poem being the vehicle by which the external / internal boundary between reality and the imagination is negotiated. For Burnside, this is 'an old reality'; something atavistic in the soul. For Stevens it is 'a new knowledge of reality'. For both, the breaking down of the internal / external binary is paramount. Jonathan Bate has also discussed Stevens' poem, noting how Stevens' poem 'belongs to the book and not the world; it is the "supreme fiction". But the poet longs to ground his being in the actualities of the world. The strivings of the imagination must be reconciled with connection to the earth' (116), a unifying philosophy that defines Burnside's own poetics, and which he will later identify in his poem 'Unwittingly' in the image of 'the lit space'.

This effectual 'striving of the imagination reconciled with connection to the earth' is further exemplified by Burnside's poem 'Like me, you sometimes waken', presented here in entirety:

Like me, you sometimes waken
early in the dark
thinking you have driven miles
through inward country,

feeling around you still
the streaming trees and startled waterfowl
and summered cattle
swinging through your headlamps.

Sometimes you linger days
upon a word,
a single, uncontaminated drop
of sounds; for days

it trembles, liquid to the mind,
then falls:
mere denotation,
dimming in the undertow of language
(*Common* 9).

The movement here is circular: from interior to exterior, to things themselves, to the words for things in language, then back into the mind as 'mere denotations', before dimming, like shadows in 'the undertow of language'. This logical shape, moving from the real into poetry, is key to Burnside's poems, such as 'Lost' in *Feast Days*. Here the poet remembers woods where he disappeared for long hours on Sunday afternoons 'looking for the lithe / weasel in the grass' (*Feast* 10). In a common device of animism, Burnside equates himself with this 'pink-toothed / killer, the casual // expert, the tribal memory of one / who slips into the chicken runs of mind' (10). There is an animal brutality, mirrored by a brooding, human 'bright rage' in this poem, characteristic of the darker, violent side of Burnside's art. What is important here is the placement of 'the mind': right at the end. What precedes it is the detail of the real world: woods, weasel, grass, tracks, sunlight, nettles. Once the imagery is established from the real world, only then do we venture into the named mind/imagination, where the fusion takes place, so that the weasel begins to work 'his way with something of my own / bright rage towards the folly of the damned' (10), in a way that is perhaps reminiscent of Hughes' poem 'The Thought Fox'.

This equating of the human self with the animal, and even with the vegetable, is evident towards the end of Burnside's novel *The Locust Room* in this passage, which describes:

that old Pictish sense of continuum, that sense of something
ancient, and, at the same time, constantly new-born in the world,
which was represented by nothing, but was present in the subtler
magic of the earth, in the glimmer and drift of reeds and salt-
grass at the tide-line, in the waves of meadowsweet that marked
a ditch, or the rings of dark grass where a fairy ring began
(*Locust Room* 215).

Paul, the central character, comes to understand that if the self or soul was
anything, it 'came from the world, that it was always changing, that it was
no more a part of the person he or his father was, than the weather' (219), an
idea echoed in Burnside's poem 'A Swimming Lesson':

Maybe it's luck, or a talent for going naked
that lets one body mingle with the stream
till fingers and eyes and even the lungs
are water. Maybe it's a gift
for transformation,
changing from child to swan at the river's edge,
from swan to fish, from fish to waterweed
(*Swimming* 26).

Here the first transformation of the self is elemental (becoming water); the
next animate (from child to swan to fish), and the last vegetal (to waterweed).
For Burnside,

So much of flesh is grass, you find yourself
In ramsons and the smell of bitter cress,
In mullein and foxgloves, lighting the summer nights,

And golden iris hanging in the porch
(*Normal* 8).

Like the snake earlier, the natural world is brought indoors from the natural
environment to the domestic environment (the porch); mirroring the move
from the real world into the thought, imagined world. The device recurs
many times, as when 'you hold the door ajar' and something comes 'inside,
in that one / moment',

more than a gust of rain, more than the wind,
more than the Halloween ghosts we might imagine.
Those animals that figure on the walls,
those creatures we imagine on the stairs
are real, and we must give them shapes and names
(*Normal* 48).

This continual to-ing and fro-ing across the boundaries and through the gaps between the two creates the sense of a persistent self – a continuum between internal and external. The rejection of this dualism is most clear perhaps at the start of the poem 'Unwittingly': 'I've visited the place / where thought begins' (31). Where is that? we ask. Outside ourselves of course, as much as within:

Pear trees suspended in sunlight, narrow shops,
alleys to nothing

but nettles
and broken walls
(*Normal* 31)

Whoever we are – and 'it may look different to you' the poet concedes – this place where thought begins is 'always the same lit space, the one good measure'. Being a lit space, it is the space in which we 'dwell'; it is both 'home' in the real world, and the home of imagination. This 'lit space' is neither necessarily inside nor outside, although it must come inside from outside, forming a continuum that 'displaces the day's / pale knowledge', making ourselves 'come to' ourselves 'in a glimmer of rainfall or frost, / the burnt smells of autumn, / a meeting of parallel lines' (32). The 'lit space' is the gap between those parallel lines; between the self and other; between internal and external; between imagination and reality; between nature and culture. It is the 'lit space' of the ecopoem – the 'strange rhetoric of the parallel between nature and the imagination' as Wallace Stevens calls it – where we dwell.

'Dwelling' is central to Burnside's long and ambitious collection of poems, *The Asylum Dance*. Of 'dwelling' Burnside says, 'I think of the discipline of poetry as a slow, lyrical, and fairly tentative attempt to understand and describe a meaningful way of dwelling in this extraordinary world' (in Crawford *Contemporary* 95). *The Asylum Dance* is characterised by the word, and revolves around four long poems – 'Ports', 'Settlements', 'Fields' and 'Roads' – which punctuate the collection and provide a spine. 'Ports' establishes the centrality of 'Our dwelling place', which is both the poet's actual home 'above the firth' in Scotland, and the ecopoetic 'dwelling place / inherent in the spine / that // kinship of flesh with flesh' (5). Dwelling is 'the painful gravity / that comes of being settled on the earth' (29) and is always negotiated through relationships with *the other*, whether the other be a lover, nature, other people, neighbours, twins, or even *things* themselves: 'the otherlife of things' as the poet writes in 'Otherlife' (42), that is to be found in the 'pull of the withheld' (*Asylum* 42). And, as we saw at the outset, Burnside's thought is rooted in a philosophy of respect for the other. And for the poet, of course, the dwelling place is inevitably also an imagined dwelling place made of words:

> no more or less correct than anything
> we use to make a dwelling in the world
> (*Asylum* 8).

If home is where we dwell, and ecopoetry is an expression of that dwelling, then John Burnside's oeuvre is a beautiful lyrical quest to 'get home' to 'the lit space' in both reality *and* imagination in which the poem becomes a fusion of the two. From the animal world, it finds its expression in 'the homing instinct', to which there are many references in his work, right the way back to his very early publication *Homing*.[3] This fusion of reality and imagination within the lit space of the lyric poem is, for Burnside, the ecopoetic form of homing

>   in the purer urgency
> of elsewhere
>   which is nothing like the mind's
> intended space
>   but how the flesh belongs
>   (*Asylum* 11).

---

[3] Published as J.P Dick. *Homing*. Menard Press

References

Bachelard, Gaston. *The Poetics of Space*. Boston: Beacon Press, 1994.

Bate, Jonathan. *The Song of the Earth*. London: Picador, 2001.

Burnside, John. *A Normal Skin*, London: Jonathan Cape, 1997.

Common Knowledge, London: Secker & Warburg, 1991.

Feast Days, London: Secker & Warburg, 1992. Reprinted 1994.

(as J.P. Dick) *Homing*. Newcastle: Menard Press, 1983.

Swimming in the Flood, London: Jonathan Cape, 1995.

The Asylum Dance, London: Jonathan Cape, 2000.

The Hoop. Manchester: Carcanet Press, 1988.

The Locust Room. London: Jonathan Cape, 2001.

The Myth of the Twin, London: Jonathan Cape, 1994.

Crawford, Robert (ed). *Contemporary Poetry and Contemporary Science*. Oxford: Oxford University Press, 2006.

Dosa, Attila. 'Poets and Other Animals: an Interview with John Burnside'. *Scottish Studies Review 4:1*, 2003 [9-23].

Stevens, Wallace. *Collected Poems*. London: Faber & Faber, 2006.

Fiona Sampson

The Expanded Lyric:
John Burnside and the Challenge to British tradition

An unintended consequence of recent interest in formalism – and of the patronage system generated by writing workshop culture – has been a straitening of poetic resources. Like the Georgian moment in early twentieth-century verse, contemporary poetry tends to contraction, in both scale and ambition. That earlier period of focus generated the lyric lucidity of Edward Thomas and, arguably, Ivor Gurney; a century later, a somewhat similar refocusing has thrown up Don Paterson and his imitators. But the very neo-Georgian virtues that distill such thrilling clarity in the hands of major poets – control, and the favouring of the recognizably local and individual over hazardous grandiosity – risk a cycle of diminishing returns among the minor talents.

Much of today's mediocre writing is in free verse yet, though it lacks the disciplined pleasures of strict form, it has internalised a principle of constraint. Like teenagers practising air-guitar in provincial bedrooms, poets who lack a true note of their own anguish over cool. They do so because of the simplification it offers the risk-averse. Since it engages with nothing it hasn't already prepared for, the 'cool' poem is unlikely to break down under an overwhelming burden of, for example, truth. Twice-rehearsed, cool verse aspires to the predictable and the known. Not only is it anti-spontaneous, and therefore to some extent resistant to every lucky, unpredictable idea, image and phrase; but its centre of gravity is normative. It aims for conformity to models that, however contemporary, do already exist.

From time to time a poetics emerges which counteracts this process of attrition with the kind of capacious generosity Les Murray calls 'sprawl', and Rostand's *Cyrano de Bergerac*, 'panache'. Bold, even radical, remedies for the lyric mainstream's flirtation with diminishing returns aren't to be found among the by-now-familiar conventions of a *soi disant* avant-garde, hedged in by rules and resistances of their own, but in a more than usually expansive occupation of the centre ground. It's this that makes the expanded lyric, developed in this country most notably by John Burnside, so significant for British poetry.

Characterized by a rangy poetic scale and wide-ranging, synthesizing intelligence, the expanded lyric tends to enter contemporary British poetry speaking with an Australian accent; although I suspect Burnside sees himself as more influenced by a North American tradition that includes figures as various, and as various in their poetic roots, as Robert Hass and Brigid Pegeen Kelly. Both inter-continental traditions belong beyond the remit of this piece, but it's important to note the context created by the exuberant eco-riffs of the hugely-productive John Kinsella. He combines profound intelligence, political conscience and a sort of Shelleyian rapture in a fast-moving hyper-lyric which prickles with detail and idea. More level in tone, but equally thoughtful and capacious, are figures like Martin Harrison; Les Murray himself has not only produced *Freddy Neptune,* a great war novel in verse, but pushes through poetic convention into a strangely literal, animist-autist view of the world.

Nevertheless, one poet does not make a revolution. Burnside's steady refusal to conform to contemporary norms has sometimes been costly. The near-visionary, mobile authority of his poetry means his large readership is a particularly dedicated one, but fewer poetry time-servers seem to have the matching courage to reward a poet who breaks ranks, and does so with deftness and generosity. This is not to suggest that Burnside is undistinguished. But he has been disproportionately, at times even scandalously, passed-over – sometimes with the whisper that 'he repeats himself'. Most poets strike a vein and continue to mine it: but Burnside's work exhibits a line of development that is in fact more pronounced than is often the case. While the early books, concerned with observation and apprehension, employed a range of forms, 2000's *The Asylum Dance* placed a kind of fractured dream-narrative centre-stage. Subsequent collections transmuted this into the evocation of experiences simultaneously spiritual and sensual, often demonstrating a heightened ecological awareness. In *Gift Songs* the same mobile intelligence dealt directly with philosophical and metaphysical questions.

What's really going on, of course, is that the work is so distinctive that it's this difference, rather than the poetry itself, which casual readers 'hear'. In the five collections published during the first decade of this century – the prize-winning *The Asylum Dance* (2000), *The Light Trap* (2002), *The Good Neighbour* (2005), *Gift Songs* (2007) and *The Hunt in the Forest* (2009) – John Burnside's project of lyric expansion is immediately visible. Long, often stepped lines, in poems that frequently work as sequences of lyric interludes, take up spacious place on the page. There's lots of white paper – air, space, resonating chamber? – and the spaces between and around the lines also suggest a page which has not been fully used up. Even at a distance, these 'early-middle' poems imply a degree of under-determination. On the other hand, they guide the eye, and in that sense 'conduct' the reader. The stepped lines, in particular, look almost like arrows:

He has come to a halt in the woods:
snow on the path
           and everything gone to ground
in its silken lair;

gone to ground
           or folded in a death
so quiet, he can almost taste the fade
of hair and vein,
           ('Saint Hubert and the Deer', 2009)

The effect of following these directions for reading is so clearly musical that we should better call them scoring.

If we pay attention to this musical logic, we find ourselves listening in on an accelerated, slippery tunefulness. The poem's central gesture is a kind of topple, something utterly removed from the level-pegging of pentameter and its equalizing tensions. John Burnside is a poet of surrender. Far from producing certainties, his poems are continually in flight from it; as if from a false consciousness. Each image is a temporary habitation for, if not meaning, then at least reflective consciousness. A passage from 'Dirt Road', the third part of 'By Pittenweem',

Something that runs to copper
or cornflower blue,

a live creature bounding away
from the glare of my headlamps

and, when the engine stops, a sudden quiet
that waits to be filled

by owls, or cicadas;
[...]

is *both* about one thing, an instant of glimpsing, *and* about a whole series of experiences – one colour, then another, 'a live creature bounding away', headlamps, sudden quiet, owls, cicadas – which can't be integrated into a single picture, but instead track the consciousness that bounds from one thing to another, the true 'live creature' of the poem.

This kind of bounding trajectory might appear to refuse the poem's basic task of unity, and it can certainly seem as if a Burnside poem also escapes from *itself;* a sensation underscored by virtuoso use of extended, sometimes poem-long, sentences. ('Dirt Road' is one; and the 'By Pittenweem' sequence as a whole contains several sentences of more than a page in length each.) But unity is not stasis, and these concertina-ing techniques heighten what we could call longitudinal unity. One part of the poem is explicitly joined to the next (couplet, stanza, phrase) by an aural logic.

In part this is achieved by the rhythmic balance phrases strike. In the opening couplets of 'Stalkers' (2009), the alternating balance of two-stress, three-stress, lines is further inflected by nursery anapests:

Tell me again
the stories you tell a child

when the season begins
and the hunters are out on the moor[.]

Often, though, that balance is less regular:

[...] That *self* is metaphor

and what he mistakes for himself
                    and the presence he loves
are different

            as emptiness and form
give rise to one another ceaselessly

the shaper shaped
            the lines identical.
            ('The Myth of Narcissus', II)

Here the to-and-fro of phrases – with lines stepped even across the stanza break – satisfies the ear because it satisfies the *sense* that ear makes. Though they aren't grammatically-independent clauses, each does represent a 'step' of understanding. In fact, the absence of active verbs from the last two phrases has a unifying effect, making them seem 'brushed in the same direction', and this sense of movement is reinforced by the oscillation at the half-line-break, where the repeated *sh/a* sounds are replaced by *is* and *ls*. The soundscape may be suddenly contrasted, but the step in the line creates a strongly eye-led here-there sense of something as much joined as separate.

This is no accident: the half-line is the secret generator of much British poetry. Its twin roots are in the assonantal forms of Anglo-Saxon and mediaeval Welsh verse, and in the parallelism of psalmody, so widely-adopted in Christian liturgy. In assonantal forms the half-line repeats the sound, in parallelism the sense, of what has just been said. Burnside's de-compressed lyric is liberated from this obligation to repeat, but retains the impetus that comes from a shared 'direction of travel'. That doubling impetus, the second bounce at the line's half-way point, also characterizes the work of poets as varied as David Harsent and Geoffrey Hill; but in Burnside's work its role is more distinctively that of accelerator, largely because his poetry strips out many of the small-scale grammatical and semantic structures, like qualifying clauses, which set up local rhythmic resistances to the line's trajectory.

But technique, even that as distinctive as Burnside's, is always instrumental. This continual longitudinal shift is reflected in the poet's characteristic chain-link imagery, which sets up a continual transfer of imagistic, and often metaphorical, currency. Conventionally, poets enter a metaphor and then leave it after a short or extended passage, closing it after them as if this were a particular kind of parenthesis that had opened up within the poem. Rather than *generating* narrative or ideational movement, the traditional metaphor drops anchor at one expository spot. By contrast, in the Introduction to his own translation of the *Duino Elegies,* that Modernist masterpiece, David Young quotes comments on Dante by Osip Madelstam, the author's Russian near-contemporary, in order to explain Rainer Maria Rilke's extraordinary strategy of making metaphors, images or ideas open out of each other:

Imagine to yourself an airplane […] which in full flight constructs and launches another machine. In just the same way this second flying machine, completely absorbed in its own flight, still manages to assemble and launch a third. […] The assembly and launching of these technically unthinkable machines […] form a most essential attribute and part of the flight itself […]

Burnside, who studied modern languages and thus has a genuinely unmediated access to European poetry, is almost the only contemporary British poet to be influenced by this non-parenthetical way of thinking through a poem. For example, in his 'Ars Moriendi…' (from 2009's 'An Essay Concerning Time'), the art of dying is 'Like going to meet a friend / […] /though no-one is there, at last, in the quiet room / that so much resembles / the room you have just abandoned': or else it – death? The room? – is like the 'space long-abandoned' of a 'hut at the end of the track / that runs through the woods' where among souvenirs 'a music that nobody hears' comes in through the open door. Each of these images – the feeling of anticipation, the empty room, the more familiar room recently left, the hut at the end of the track, the unheard, mysterious music – is both a direct metaphor for death, linking back to the start of the thought-sequence, and a simile for its own immediate precursor in this daisy-chain of descriptive logic.

Burnside's insights are both evanescent – beautiful almost before we understand what they mean – and evasive, a recurring fantasy of escape through dissolution: 'the shift / from here to there, from near to almost gone' ('Kronos', *op cit*). They portray a world of flux and dream. The sources of this world-view may be as various as drug culture (as his second volume of memoir, *Waking up in Toytown*, suggests) or scientific ideas of flux and contingency, but Burnside is also taking up a position in relation to meaning-making. A profound anti-dogmatism characterizes his work. Like much secular spirituality his ecological, almost-pantheistic spirituality is un-doctrinal, not to mention anti-doctrinaire. His poems rarely state what they believe, or arrive at conclusions either narrative or intellectual. Like the 'Essays' of *The Hunt in the Forest*, the major, multipartite 'Responses' and 'Four Quartets' of *Gift Songs* – his most explicitly theological and philosophical book to date – are expansive explorations rather than narrowing processes of examination and conclusion. In this, he is part of a wider tradition. In late-Modern European philosophy, both Friedrich Nietzsche and Martin Heidegger struggled against an automatic belief in the veracity of labels: what their inheritor Jacques Derrida would call a 'metaphysics of presence'.

Their prose tied itself in knots (or nots) in its attempt to avoid treating language as 'true'. Burnside's poetry, by contrast, is unknotted and jargon-free, but it does allow us to glimpse how words might be contingent, fleeting devices for dealing with the world. Composing 'on the ear', he is a Shelleyian whose strategic evocations of speed bring together the flux and contingency of the world and of experience. That poetry must be in and of its world, and the world it responds to is unstable, is of course a Modernist apprehension. But if Percy Bysshe Shelley was in some ways neo-Modernist, John Burnside is in his own manner a late Romantic, who looks to his own responses to replace both an absent God and the Realist contract. So what happens if he seems to return, as he does in *Black Cat Bone* (2011), to more apparently-conventional verse-forms? There are fewer stepped lines in this collection, and some poems – 'The Listener' and the stanzaic 'Pieter Brueghel: Winter Landscape with Skaters and Bird Trap, 1565' (printed in this issue) – are baldly columnar, in a way that almost seems like an exasperated challenge to conservative readers, as if the subtle delineation of half-line breaks had been crudely redrawn by yoking everything back to the left-hand margin:

[...] something like the absence of ourselves
from our lives,
some other luck
that would not lead
to now.
and:
The long-dead blanking the roads
and everything
disloyal to the earth
it came from [...]
                    ('The Listener')

The forty-one very short lines of the single-sentence 'Amnesia' seem to mimic the 'squeeze' on a (lost) memory, and the narrowing of attention in the snow-bound world in which the poem is set.

But couplets and tercets haunt the book, holding out a false promise of simplification. The hinged poems of 'The Nightingale' use couplets to evoke the kind of orderly, two-by-two discussion that attempts to work out what's going wrong in a marriage:

I come home late and vanish on the stairs;
you riffle through the Deaths and Marriages

for something more akin
to passion spent,

and when you leave me so,
unsatisfied,

I lumber on by mutual consent
[...]

As though this psycho-drama is too richly-complex to lie down within parallel lines, the poem's second section is also haunted by a running, irregular end-rhyme – *rent/mezzotint/Lent/spent/consent/ascent* – that generates a sense of uncanny, inevitable or perhaps uncomprehended fit.

The book's two most significant poems, though, are both in tercets. Of these the long, five-part, introductory poem, 'The Fair Chase' (also printed in this issue), is a cross between ballad and folk-tale, in which the protagonist, a sort of holy fool – 'flycatcher, dreamer, dolt, /companion to no one, /alone in a havoc of signs' – observes the hunting traditions of family and community, and 'becomes / the thing he kills'. This kind of transubstantiation isn't new in Burnside's work, but its explicitly *narrative* working-out, calling as much to Ovid as to Ferenc Juhász, the Brothers Grimm as to his own distinguished parallel career as a novelist, is a seam he has left largely untouched in verse since the title poem of *The Asylum Dance*. That much-shorter poem, written a decade earlier and based on blank verse, shares a narrative structure with 'The Fair Chase': after the crisis of a life-changing encounter comes the extended, dream-like afterlife, with its longing for reprise. Burnside's 'honey-slick', 'pearl-effect' sensibility is well-adapted to this kind of poetics of regret.

Yet *Black Cat Bone*'s most important departure is what we might call its title poem – at least, the poem in which the Black Cat Bone makes its appearance – the thirteen-line 'Hurts Me Too'. It's tempting to call every expanded lyric 'exploded', since the centrifugal principle of explosion does imply a continuing relationship with a central 'spine' of form. But certainly, if this love-poem is a sonnet, whose opening declaration, *I love my love with an X*, is repeated at the traditional point of sonnet turn, it is one that has been exploded. Its dispersed sense, in the second stanza for example –

> Rain on the yards; a cuckoo in the meadows;
> I look in my bed tonight
>   and find
> my brothers and sisters gone

– is retroactively gathered to the explosive point of the last line:

> she thinks [my mouth] is safe
>   until I drink her in.

Something has broken through both form and register, and the stippled imagery and gracious music of much of Burnside's earlier verse falls away at this blunt touch. In its last phrase, we overhear the potential for a whole new way of writing.

John Burnside's lyric expansiveness is articulated by much more than just his readily-visible stepped lines. His twelve collections to date include conventionally-shaped verse and prose poems. The school of expanded lyricists which is only now emerging is influenced by the whole of this work, not merely that from the first decade of this century. Perhaps it has taken so long for this group to emerge because Burnside's project is as thorough-going and radical as Anthony Caro's has been within British sculpture. To join multiple impulses to each other, as Caro started to do in the sixties with pieces such as the famous straggling red forms of 'Early One Morning' (1962),

119

rather than focus on a single principle as sculpture and the lyric has largely done, requires an audience with expectations as new as those of the artist. Whatever the reason, it is very new poets, like Maitreyabandhu and Aviva Dautch, and the secular visionaries Alan Stubbs and David Briggs, whose work most distinctively exhibits the kind of scope – in theme, flexibility of image and movement of thought – Burnside 'permits'.

Although it's early to know whether, and how, their work will develop, Dautch and Maitreyabandhu, both writing from – and *of* – a faith background (Dautch trained as a rabbi, Maitreyabandhu runs the London Buddhist Centre) are particularly Burnside-ian in their use of the suspended phrase and floating imagery so useful for characterizing the underdetermined nature of spiritual enquiry. Maitreyabandhu has also learnt from Burnside's use of colour and his unexpected, almost category-busting, similes for mood or feeling:

just there

like the shadow of a church

or a quiet brother.
And how I saw you, in the mess of things,
was as a slant of grey,
the perfect grey of house dust,
an absolute neutral, with no weaving,
no shimmer of cobalt
and light-years away from Byzantium.
('Visitation')

But both have also been exposed to other influences that might lead to writing of this sort. Maitreyabandhu takes part in the 'floating world' of Buddhist meditation, chant and scripture; Dautch refers to French feminists like Hélène Cixous, with their 'strategy of celerity', not to mention a wider international tradition of Jewish women writers including poets, like Gloria Gervitz in Mexico and the Sardinian Antonella Anedda, who are concerned with rapture.

These parallel influences remind us that Burnside himself is part of a long, and broad, poetic tradition. Paul Celan's European heirs, descending by way of Ingeborg Bachmann, are highly significant but, since largely-female, often overlooked as an international school: they include the Slovak Mila Haugova, a major figure in Central Europe, and Claire Malroux in

France.[1] Like Burnside, these poets lean against the circumscribing line of the traditional boxed-in lyric, though the phrases with which they break it open are explicitly lyrical.

Such peers also remind us that, while British poets who try to adopt certain of Burnside's strategies as a *style* are acknowledging his influence – whether consciously or not – they aren't engaged in the same poetic *project*. Since her 2003 collection *Minsk,* Lavinia Greenlaw has experimented with liminal themes – a Burnsidean landscape of estuaries in her sequence 'Winter Finding' – and suggestive remission from regular metres. Others to hazard this borrowed style include Philip Gross, who mimics 'The Language of the Bird People' in *The Wasting Game.* Frances Presley, Janet Sutherland and other poets with a background in more radical tradition have experimented the half-line breath, expressed as a space rather than a step. But in the work of all these poets, these techniques become principles of contraction, a licence for the tentative note rather than the horizon-defying exuberance which marks Burnside's contribution:

> [...] for you
> the light at the end of the tunnel is never quite air,
>
> and breath is a shape that sails out over the rooftops,
> into the lights off the quay and the tethered yawls.
> ('In Memoriam')

---

[1] I guess I might belong, distantly, to this tradition myself, and certainly my experience suggests that it's difficult to do so in Britain.

Lynne Wycherley

The Shell Man

Robert Rendall on Birsay

Imagine his world –
seals on the taing,
the flicker of the burn,
its chamfered stones

and this: a cold hollow,
a Moebius curve,
its infinity
cupped in his hand.

Near-deaf, he listens
through touch,
rides the whelk's spiral,
the clefs of the sea.

He'll taste the names,
test vowels on his tongue,
cornelets, tiger-scallop,
tellins, and they'll

take him beyond
our bones' frail house –
blue-rayed limpets
with pale ochre skies,

the spectrum
of *Faroese sunsets* –
to the sea's 'Te Deum',
the horizon's trance.

Westray Firth

We are alone in lit silver.

Terns dance
their thin certainties,

the wind's grey hand
worries the shine

and I do not know
what draws me more –

the gull-picked green
of the waiting shore

or Rousay receding,
rock made air,

blue solutes
melting in blue.

A Distance Lit with Deer

(for Ian)

You wade far out
as the hedgerows wake,
serins rustling their shadows,
as slow light comes in eddies
over the fields

and there they are: the deer,
warm pigments in hyacinth.
Heads raised,
hooves poised
on the point of flight,

kinetic. Counterparts
of your cut-loose self,
miles from database, city.
Time after time
you see them,

a brace, a dozen
while I dream –
henna and haem, electrostatic
in the light-tipped grass,
their limber backs
                    hovering.

Groom to bride,
you turn to our house,
a supple pace,
the grace of fire, as you
carry them home in your stride.

Winter Trees

Black wicks in a burning sky,
they stood on the rim of our senses
where the garden fell to fields.
I'd see them from a low window,
thin sentries in threadbare light
glimpsed over scrapbooks, crayons,
a bear with a cinnabar eye.

By semis, C-roads, paths caked
with snow, their branches rise.
Linear in aquatint, a crisp ink
on shell-tints and whey; birch-twigs
and sallow, mespil and lime.
Dusk sinks: they soar. Through them
I face the vehement stars,

voids of space, annihilation
by ice and fire. Dear trees,
yours is the first inscription
and the last. The whittled sky
recedes; returns. Faint
emanations of coral, fawn,
cradled in the uplift of your arms.

Tim Murdoch

Home Ground

The question doesn't answer.
It only drives on deeper
and fills us, motionless,
to the brim of its cup.

We've slowed to the place
where you feel for an hour
I've left you; where at last
you know that we touch.

Reading Elizabeth Smart

My nerves fizzled, recognizing
their mysterious benediction...

I'd only got as far as verse two
but had to stop, to gaze upwards
from the basement courtyard
of my cousin's flat, as rain fell
through a small rectangular sky
down onto page, cheek and table.

You were moved to love by reading
the tender words of another poet.
What moved me was having to
abandon my reading altogether;
look how water freshens the air
and streaks my old linen jacket.

The Gate

Before you died, one morning early
we made contact. In my waking dream
I saw you tired, your steps faltering –
though you'd never as yet appeared so –
in need of my help to throw salt into
a bank of snow piled against a heavy gate
you were ready to unlatch.

A week later, still a hundred miles away,
my brain went quiet. I had to stop the car
and sit awhile, not thinking why.
Out of the blue, my companion asked
what my mother would do if my father died.
Back in Shepton Montague, a call
came through. The gate was open.

The Disappearance

Night waves were our metronome,
then as day was waiting to breathe
you took my hand to the soft high
meadow of your reclining body
and together, steadily, we carried
our new boat down to the tide
which lifted us, thoughtlessly,
caring not how, why or whither.

We'd said, of course, in a
moment of high-alert mortality,
defending our rigorous belief,
that this would not be a way home.
But it was, even this, and there
wasn't a soul about to argue.

Eleanor Hooker

The Island

So humid, even the wooden bannisters sweat.
Out on the island woodpeckers headbutt Alder trees,
Like shocked heartbeats, the rapid *lub-dub lub-dub*

Will find its echo in me. My dog laps water,
Making delicious sounds, delicious thirst-quenching sounds.
Her tongue hangs long, quivering, stretched to tear.

'Close your mouth.' I say, as I launch Kibihee. The boathouse is cool,
Air soothed in sponged light. Kibihee's timbers sigh against the blue
Tickle of water. In this summer heat as I oar us out of depth,

The shoreline shimmers unsteadily and when the engine coughs
We are underway at last. The Island's trees are lined with birds,
Heraldic wings outstretched drying in the sun,

A cormorant arboretum. They choir a deep harsh croak,
A cacophony of dissent at our approach. But they know well
We will not be turned; we mean to find a way onto the island.

I cut the motor and on the breeze Kibihee drifts closer
To the rocky shore. The movement of swans in ballet
Overhead is like a warning sign.

Another summer I would have left, but not today.
Though more and more birds arrive, today I hold my nerve.
One by one cormorants come to greet me, landing on the gunwale,

Their backward-forward toes gripping Kibihee. This is what
I've waited for, my 'come-true story' and one I've heard every summer
Of my life from my Granddad. Lifted from the water,

My boat protests her age. Alarmed by the creaking of her planks,
I shift my weight as we are settled quite steady, in the steady quiet
Of a summer oak, deep, deep within the island,

A hidden place, where not looking would find
That looking would not find me. 'For how long?' Sasha asks.
Inside this island dogs talk and cormorants know the limit of fear.

This is where trees walk to the water's edge
To watch sailors fumble with the wind and bow at trees
On the opposite shore, rooted there forevermore.

'For just today' I say. To the arrhythmic drumbeat from my heart,
We are rocked asleep inside a dream of Kibihee being rocked asleep
Inside a dream. And when I awake, I'll know its time.

Singing Ice

Across the rigid icescape they heave
And haul colossal cables to the shadows
On the opposite shore. We shudder at the echoing
Crack and coil of tensile steel on the cold lid of winter.

Back and forth the spectres murmur.
We hear them hum the hymns of the dead;
Ceremonial chants that rise and fall for hours,
That gathering volume, resonate like breathless

Air across empty glass. We venture out a foot or so.
Beneath us air-sharks drop and dive through
Slivers of thickening water, then rise to slam
The frozen under-surface. They tear long rips

That roar along the night, tracking us and splitting
The marbled floor at our feet. The percussions
Petrify the living and the dead sing on.

Chris Hardy

Momentarily Bright

Kingfisher in the evening
    a blue beam
flicking on in the dark
    tree-tunnel
above a stream.

The bird
    momentarily bright
made us wait
    but did not return
hidden by the dark
    pouring down
through leaves
    and drowning sight.

We cut back
    through trackless wheat
trusting the bird's
    blue searchlight
would show the way
    as it still does
treading down this
    forgotten day.

Maitreyabandhu

Puja

The 'worth' you're looking for
in 'worship' – this puja –

is beyond the goat bells
on the mountain ridge,

the valley running softly,
your own difficult heart.

You have to face into it,
putting out your hands.

And you might have used
his name or made a picture –

a face, perhaps his face
looking back at you – or you

might have chosen words.
You know it's not the usual

silence, after the dragonflies
have gone, after you've eaten –

but you're afraid, now
you turn to look, that you'll

keep missing it and missing it.

The Master

The wind dies in the larches – a gust takes them,
        rocks them,

     then slows everything to a standstill:
          Grandma holding the boys,
your father by the tool shed,
        Stephen standing by the dodgems
          waiting for you to speak.

You have to find the one who's always outside,
          always stepping down,
    but you only have pictures
      to go on,
          pictures covered with tracing paper.

You wish you were standing on the Mount.
        You wish it had snowed
and you were taking the dogs out –
     Ajax scenting a rabbit,
        your breath making plumes.
But you can't imagine it,
    skirting the church
      where your parents walked
        under an avenue of cricket bats.

You can see the path
      leading past the graveyard where your grandmother
        wouldn't have a stone,
   you can see St Nicholas' and St John's –
       the edge of your roof,

     the whole of Brookend Drive –
but you can't see him:
       the Master of Minnows and Crayfish.

Samantha Wynne Rhydderch

Dressmaking

They might have thought she was dead,
the sailors, as they docked opposite her door,
as if some trick of the light

would dupe them into seeing her propped
in a black box by the stove, but truly she'd be
dictating stitches whilst they crossed

the quay tilting cheap coffins and tea chests
onto the waiting carts. The date of her daughter's
birth was the last thing she'd written

in thread, an epitaph before paralysis
struck. *Cut it on the bias* she'd call,
tack it back as the little girl's fingers

clipped the fabric, felt it fall to a floor
numb with her mother's sprinkled pins.

Emigré

Let me cradle its stiff body
one more time before I lay it

in a velvet bed. I've no mind to pin
its strings to the fingerboard
or coax the blond hair of a bow
over its bony shoulders, this the only

companion of your narrow bunk
in steerage on the voyage out

and on the barstool down the cobbled lane
where you sank your last glass
of Porter the hour you boarded,
at one with the swing of the ship,

tapping out a waltz in two four time
in tune with the engine's crooning.

So when you replied to her notice
in the Purser's office: *Wanted: a sea-flute,
apply Emma Lewis* you made music
all the way to Ellis Island yet I am

custodian all the way back of your silent
violin and this, a doll-sized coffin.

Delft

I promise when I pack up your clogs,
raise them to chime with one chipped toe
your passing; when I glue back a pleat
in the skirt of the lady with pale blue hair
whose apron said 'Bugge' after she fell
down the stairwell revealing a bell
beneath her dress on which a windmill
waved goodbye to the flight of four birds
reflected in the inky water; when I wrap
the cold tile where your butter flattened
the sheaves of hay combed to a tuft
in the still wind in which etched-in cows
stared out under the low clouds looming over
the walled garden whose gate I longed to
walk through always, the glaze will be wet
on all your Delft, on both my hands.

Gypo

The turquoise eyes of peacocks' tails
at Powis Castle persuaded me
that pattern matters. So did the geometry
of pink brick twisted chimneys

at Compton Wynyates in whose
knot gardens I found myself
lost and intricate at eight. I'd
memorise visors and Gothic screens,

gables and displays of tapestries.
I could tell a Pembroke
from a Pier table, played
Greensleeves on the recorder,

cupped the faces of misericords
like much-loved dolls in places
where I did not live but visited
in the pages of *Treasures of Britain*

on a fold-out table in the caravan
I grew up in on the outskirts
of Burnley. In love with the symmetric
pleading of sleeping knights

brass-necked down to their
pointy toes, I'd design chevrons
for my family shield, draw
the Queen's buckskin boots

and virginals, squeeze myself into
the chicken run to check I'd still
fit, dreamed one day I'd own a
Ha-ha. Ha ha ha ha ha ha.

Alan Stubbs

Woken

Us
wakes me.

I picture a crow, or some dishevelled bird
alone on the roof
a fledgling perhaps
sobbing for company
that not having taken to wing
is frightened of falling
and abandoned
must consider that step into nothing
but air

there are four boats and her

they are hollowed out and gaily painted half eggshells all
too delicate in their ribbings to be let to sea in the skirmishing
winds, and have been pulled up onto sandy ridges
to rest a safe distance from the sucking lips at the water's edge.

they are allowed the journeys of small children
perhaps slipping out to as far as the new marina where
the shiny metallic cabin cruisers are, and back,
and they can be abandoned here safely without a
thought that they might be taken away, swallowed up, or disappear.

the beach is the colour of peach flesh muted by a thin dust
layer, and the sea is a blue felt flecked with grey. She

faces out to sea, and
is a broad curvy pole that the flags of black taffeta skirt and dark hair
are anchored to. She

is the only person in view. Her
shadow, and that of each row-boat, roots the shifting grains
of the soft beach that ripple in waves. There is

something unreal about the boats, as if they are models,
sketches for the real thing, or insubstantial in some way, but she

is darker than her shadow, and is
strong shoulders, torso, hips and legs all alert to changes
happening
in the waves, and in the skies shifting and blowing
that would trick the seas up into plays
of whites, and darken with threats of grey

watery depths, and she stands resisting all the spits
and pellets the wind raises, shields her face, and looks
out towards what is coming in
behind the clouds, and waits

Gary Allen

Mexico

That was the year of Mexico
tar melted in every street
fires were started along the embankments
of the motorways, cars swerved to avoid stones
and the talk was of Pele

but the shadows were long on the pavements
milk curdled like blood
front doors were propped open by panting dogs
and everything slowed to the sound of the televisions
the far off slam of a train door
of feet running in the next town down the line

like a serial saint who is lost
but is watched as an ant in a glass-case:
my father went to Donegal,
Bury my heart at Wounded Knee
or just South of Buncrana on the Derry road –

he came back late with a blackened eye
and two space guns that shot sparks:
Watch which house they go to –
she poured us lemonade as we watched Germany,
Take care on the way back up the estate,
they'll be waiting with sticks and bottles.

It's the silence you remember, after the cheers
have died away, and the heat trickles like fear
down your spine, to the only exit
and the burned-out shell of a car
the kerbs painted like far mile-stones

as a helicopter settles in the clear sky
and Jesus is beaten for a faith he is not sure of
but becomes a reluctant martyr
in the dust and the broken glass:
who won that year, in the bullring in the sun?

just the same, no one is there at the time of their death
and the evening becomes bruise purple
above the timber-yard
the ragged clouds like flags of smoke
on the far skyline, in another country.

Back Roads

I know a place that isn't on any map
or measured by a mile stone
or fenced by a triangulation point –

on summer evenings, clouds of black midges play
around the ditch pines
above the stagnant water of the dark bog-land

and it is quiet, as the sun goes down
local people walk other roads
local people are superstitious

believe that those who break the circle
come back when they die
to answer for what they have done

and there are things to find
if you dig into the moss bank
a twisted piece of steel comb

a fragment of bone too small
to be swept into a plastic-bag
shoe leather, button, bent coin, the torn heart

of a playing-card that has survived
the fire heat, the petrol heat, the sunlight
wind, rain, hail

and the locals say, You notice
how the bridge hill dips
has settled to a permanent crater?

Pine-cones fall like thunder-claps
to bounce across the road
telegraph-poles lean together from the soft earth

carrying electric whispers on the charged air –
local people say, when the breeze is right
you can hear a work-van approaching.

Jennie Osborne

Wheal Betsy

i

(mine workings, Dartmoor, West Devon)

This is a broken place
earth's bones hacked at, blown apart
plundered for their marrow

a place of hot and cold
of dank, of water ooze and drip
of hot fuse, hot spark, blast and blood

of broken men
of bones at angles
under granite

crimson in the skull
as lungs strain
air runs thin

nothing is written in straight lines here
history crooked
as a flawed seam

ledgers balanced
in the graveyard

cracked and scattered
gutted of gear and tackle
the place of breaking
broken open.

ii

You don't see the whole picture
at first

Wheal Betsey has faces
she doesn't show

You might spot a window
high up under the roofline

holding a darkness
that doesn't belong in daylight

Come at it from another angle

notice the pitted stonework
rough under your fingers

see spaces
where metal used to hang

a suggestion of cogs and wheels
that aren't quite there

Whichever way you come at it

let the wind guide you
to the frequency

snatches of bal-maidens singing
clatter of pick and pail

rough greetings   underground banter
iron scaffold creaking   grinding

Half close your eyes

Can you see the grey line trudging?
Flash of red kerchief?

Door to the underworld
banging shut?

India Russell

The Hand of Ore

Henrik Ibsen

He said it was
An ice-hand that had gripped his heart
On that chill eminence
When, finally, he'd ventured
From the fastness of his dreams
Into the darkening Winter night of
Unforgiving snows.

Out into the white, still, stretching landscape of his vision
Freezing his dreams of being once again
The honoured leader of the bank,
A king of wealth and riches,
Begged on bended knee to come back to his post,
Begged to be the conqueror he really was,
Lord of all the ènchained realms beneath the mountains,

The realms from whence the voices came,
Those voices he'd first heard within the bank vaults
Calling him to set them free, the
Spirits of the Ores beneath the earth,
Calling him with such encapturing enchantment
That all else had fallen dead before
Their Hadean song – his love, compassion, honour,
His own life.
John Gabriel Borkman was *bergtatt*.

Confident he would regain his kingdom
All through that time he 'died' –
The long dark years' imprisonment for using
Clients' wealth to gain yet more to set the spirits free –
He visualised his welcome back into his rightful world,
Rehearsed how he would stand and
Courteously receive the anxious emissaries of the bank
Requesting him with humble deference to take his post again,

144

How, nobly upright, he would incline his head and
Graciously address them and then generously accept;
Saw, once again, how he would soar
Above his magic mountains and hear their
Cònfined spirits singing up to him.

And that last night, surveying the cold, ranging realms
He was about to master, that time he died,
Crying in the stillness of the Winter night, out to the
Subservient spirits he would have freed,
'I love you, you life-craving assets – I love, love, love you!'
John Gabriel Borkman seemed a visionary.

But Ella knew he was a man condemned,
She whose love he had so coldly sacrificed
To his more powerful love of the 'bound millions',
She knew and understood and mourned.

He said at first it was an ice-hand that had
Gripped his heart
But it was a hand of ore
                  that killed him.

The Handkerchiefs

As a little girl, I believed it,
Walked along the hollyhock-edged path
In crinoline and bonnet,
Birds floating in an azure sky,
The little green gate leading to a world
Where the embroidery did not go;

But my imagination did as, gazing on the
Handkerchiefs in their cardboard box,
I inhabited that magic garden,
And, hollyhock-high,
Surrounded by its secret airs,
I wandered in a paradise.

And suddenly, today,
That glimpse of home returns,
The breath of flowers is borne upon the air
The green beyond is vibrant;
And though the lace is torn now, the
Lawn delicate with age, I know the garden
Is not mere embroidery.

Siân Thomas

This House Runs Backwards

Listen to that irregular click, that out-breathing,
unwinding wind, that widdershinning,
teeth-catching snap. Press your ear to the almost
inaudible tick. Press your cheek to a cog. Feel it dip,
chilly as brass. See windows flap open, hinges unscrew,
curtains dishevel their hems, floorboards flip dolls
into trunks with unlockable lids, and patches of sunlight
run down the walls. See in the fridge the cheese
re-curdling; knives and forks in the slow-turning
kitchen whipping to the Aga to smelt. And this sucking
thing at the letterbox is the past's mouth. It comes
with a tongue to lick oil off the mechanism.

Leaf House

Turn these pages with care: the page you have passed
buries its readers. We stand in its doorways,
lie in beds, pressed with our spines in the centre,
our stems browning. Turn with care: roll onto your mate.
The pages shut you together. The years are passing,
your bends end in seizures, in creases and groans.
Watch your hips. Turn with care: see other homes,
other inhabitants stroking the paper as you stroke
your sheets, the weft of a carpet, the relief of a carving –
three men drinking beer in an inn while the forest
looks on, clothing the tables in the shadows of trees.

Omar Sabbagh

Still In The House Of My Father

Watch where they leap, *sea-sprinters!*
And the sunny air as their blessed hinge…

Dolphins, grey and blue and innocent,
Their long noses especially meant
To scent where the wine-dark sea bends
To the low-lying, murky corridors
Of the black-backed, white-bellied sharks…

And what if I were to run, tandem with the sea,
Tandem with the moon –
Would I know where the bane lurks,
Where the boon?

Would I be one of the telling questions?
The ones that get the water to give up its salt?
The ones, by the shore, the crabs' claws seem to pray for,
Twisted as they are, crawling jagged as they are?

My sight reaches that far
Only in the house of my father,

Guided by a simple, licit star
And a sprawling awry cursive
Of hurting crimson letters.

My House

In a time of hunters and gatherers,
When a brawny arm was as valid as a tooth,
I offered her my love

And waited for the surge in her olive
Eyes; but nothing could soothe
Her witch's icy, slicing anger.

She was cold on the ache of my heart,
Her tongue's wild accent skewing my art.

Let ice sleep with ice then,
Deaf ear with deaf ear,
Tongue shattered and scattered
In its native mouth...

These words comprise my brawn
And remain: square pillars of my house.

The Lighthouse Of Four Fists

As if I could steer the night
from this deep blue cursive,
the trip of these jagged spiders,
this vain and shorter life;

as if I were perfect,
square jawed, square-set
and potent as a god,
wheeling free-boned at a wheel,
giving pain and tantrums loci like
a slim line
of lush white shingle;

as if I could begin again in
the grit and clasp of the middle,

the sky an open door, unending,
and sultry jasmine scents
for the harlequin I swore
I'd become, blending
word with word, lit-up,
singing and sending
what is sent

under four fists of fatherhood.

Patricia McCarthy

A Different Lodging

I see you no longer indoors in the pink velvet chair
where your presence remained ages after the armchair

had gone. I bump into you in blue moons only
when you skirt around me with the exaggerated footwork

from your youth of some ballroom dance wrong-learned.
You bow low as a courtier in your haste to retreat

from me, your faint words coated in hollow greetings,
non sequiturs; in your eyes that avoid mine: a hearse.

Hints of you persist, though, in stirrings underground
every season. In the front garden the snowdrops line up

gifted with immortality despite yew needles pushing them
down, their stems spindly miracles of resistance in blizzard

and driving rain. The irises have re-appeared dipped
in their own blue ink, jolting the vellums of memory.

After a three-year gap, the swallows swoop
to their nests in the same stable rafters as before. They loop

over the mare's back, droppings splashed like whitewash
for old-fashioned luck down the cobwebbed wall.

The swifts, your favourites, silenced under the black realm
of crows, shriek again between houses with a rapture

once ours. Rooms within rooms fold into a concertina pressed
in and out of the lath and daub by my banished bridal selves.

You, too, could be a revenant, in the pink velvet chair,
half-strange in your new dwelling of being, without me.

In the time we stopped, I offer you my hand – boned,
weatherings smoothed – for a tea dance.

Tinkling the Keys

Play through me gently with the best of yourself
as long ago when, a young bride and groom,
we swayed to your pub favourites, jazz

and honkey-tonk. We sang, also, in harmony,
to your fingers which flew of their own accord
across ivories, fluent and sure of their dexterity.

Play through me sadly, summoning the wild roses
on pergolas, the logs flaming into rainbow colours
granted fleetingly by grace – and forget the rest:

those hammers of Thoth struck against our skins
from warped strings, the chords reluctant to resolve
which banged off keys, disturbed in their din.

Play through me by ear, still, that I might admire
your accomplishment while I practise haltingly
from manuscripts you did not need, yellowed now,

corners torn from too many turnings in lessons:
preludes, waltzes, sonatas receding into a silence
that stuns metronomes, inhibits expression.

Play through me by heart. As reflections re-appear
in the mahogany, let me sway once more
to your medley, caught in the octaves of gorse-light

spanned by your hands. Tuners under the lid
muffle old time-signatures, lock us out from performing
duets from distances, *presto*, as time's recitative bids.

Play through me gently, sadly, by ear and by heart,
composing a counterpoint to melodies of wind,
flock, wave for the gaps on staves of our two parts.

Terry Jones

Grand

You don't play a note, not on that piano, over
and over it plays itself all from a memory,

strings and hammers strings and hammers.

Home to flies bright as rings, sharp mouse bones,
tops of bluebottles. Black as a coffin.
From scores of webs the spiders shout out,

strings and hammers strings and hammers.

Wild as genius a bird flew in, rayed its fingers
in mortified music soft and loud, cried its prison.

Stiff-backed my grandmother sat the living wire,
her ribs hummed with war sang with thunder,
she came down hard on her blue daughters
dark cherries of their eyes glistening

strings and hammers strings and hammers.

Not its music's yellow as an old rudder.
Step up most reflectively, raise elbows, flex fingers,

strings and hammers strings and hammers.

Fields

I think he's preparing for it or being prepared:
one of his eyes, he says, is sticky as egg,
hardly opens in the morning, the other is filmed
like grease-proof, world receding in mistiness;

153

he holds the newspaper at arm's length,
damns low energy bulbs, the frail, hesitant light.
Peering at the window he says fields look white:
I tell him they are white, white with ten degrees of frost,

white with the coldest winter for over a hundred years,
that in some places blackbirds have fallen frozen
from air, that a river has locked itself still as a long mirror,
and a village in the north is bound fast in snow,

every drifted street, each house thrilled to solitude.
He nods, turns back to the paper, its invisible silent columns,
stares from a distance, a survey from the air:
but I know, and he knows, as we sit together in half-light,

we are not now, never were, talking about the same fields.

Arrangement

You dropped your black cardigan right by the bay window:
it lies with its sleeves wrapped, a shadow hugging itself
or headless black swan where you stepped out of one thing

into another. It is a clue I should be able to read:
unilluminated, I gather inklings and omens like kindling.
But you are on the move – shifting between rooms,

ducking under doors, through walls, as if the house were a forest.
Now it looks like a bat – its ears, little teeth. It might crawl
deliberately towards the kitchen, look for somewhere to hand

the ink reflection of itself, its pall of dark smoke. Listen.
I won't pick it up. If you are going to shed your skin, take off
to the dark, I'll follow suit, shrug off this white shirt,

arrange it carefully by like an echo.

Christopher Crawford

Prayer to Burns

Ah Rab, I feel I'm talking to God, if only
because we've not spoken much before. If once
folk laughed at you for the weaknesses
I don't find to be weaknesses, except the one –
the women – they'd put you on the front
pages for it now. You, pissed out of
your skull, flashbulbed, rolling out a nightclub, a gorgeous
bird with her nose in your armpit, leaving poetry
to fuck itself for the night while you take solid
flesh and eat it like a pear. Farmer, layabout, poet,
show me again how the Scots can do it all.
Renaissance men, autodidacts, ploughers
of the sweetest parts of the earth, how we shoulder
off the laughter of those who can fly but cannot
ever land. Show me, show me again, I've forgotten.

Mark Totterdell

Sea Wall

Observe
hunks of limestone, hand-hewn, smoothed
by waves, variously
dove-grey, mauve, tinged with pink,
or like a sky with quartz con-trails;
eggshell-textured, or printed with
the frail enduring forms
of colonial creatures from the
Carboniferous.

Attend
hints of rainbow plumage in the gaps
between planks; keratin scratches,
flecks of white, the flutterings
and cooings that suggest a kind of
columbarium.

Above a scalloped, wind-sculpted sea,
fall-streaks are clusters of feathers.
Reflect
by what apparent miracle
the coral of the brain makes
correspondences.

Warren Stutely

october windows   west wight

a pewter wave
            of fish
waking a silence
            of virgil in pure
            spilt
latin
scrawls in black
            bright ink

miraculous october windows
                        white
as ordained bowls
            liquid
an inland of
            swift morning syllables

shallow and pearl drenched
                        coastal grey
dreams itself
            a trick of shell sounds

in whiter archaeologies
                        than the first
psalming
day of white

            water vessels lip
and feather grey water garments

            shock a glassy
coastal sigh thistling
            so grey aquiline above angels

birdswoop grey
            quill scripts a distance
of rain fragment

              sky   washed
                                  at its birth
of gull grey
                  nimble histories

marsh
silver
                  inching to a
gift of eyes
                  in their moist
            light
                         senses

grey of the
              word
                              heaven
            ward

a gull ritual
         thirsts
                              sea
         pebble
                         grey

october charts
                     simplicities
epistles
            in fish charms   and all
grey
becomings

the world
            is discovered

Harry Guest

Her Secret Valley

Flows down the slope towards a distance
barred by long hills and inaccessible.
From here, standing in an upper room,
you can't decipher any starting-point
past terracotta roofs and a few conifers.
It's at its best at evening when here
and there along its unknown length gold lights
prick on, holding an appeal at other hours
by staying unattainable. A strip of land.
Not one of no return nor out of bounds.
Contained by mystery not barbed wire. Absent
from every chart. Spread of a pale green field.
No hint of roads. Hard to make out, one far
grey wall seems to have lancet windows.
No sign of movement caught at any time.
Intriguing trees. To stroll beneath them though
would never do. Never be possible.
That valley lies beyond analysis –
somewhere she owns in depth of mind as real
as any yard or pavement nearer by
but not to be worked out through calculation.
Nor unmasked.

Peter Sirr

Age of the duck-hare: the poetry of Valerio Magrelli

Valerio Magrelli, *The Embrace: Selected Poems*, translated by Jamie McKendrick, Faber and Faber, 2009 (published in the US by Farrar, Strauss and Giroux as *Vanishing Points*); *Nearsights*: Selected Poems by Valerio Magrelli, edited and translated by Anthony Molino, Graywolf Press, 1991; Valerio Magrelli, *The Contagion of Matter*, translated by Anthony Molino, Holmes and Meier, 2000.

Valerio Magrelli is one of the brightest stars of Italian poetry, widely acclaimed since the appearance of his first collection *Ora Serrata Tesserae* when he was twenty three. The title of that collection gives a hint of the kind of poet he is – it's the irregular, serrated demarcation between the retina and the circumferential tissue inside the eye. So specialist is the title that when he went to the optician some months after the book came out, the optician remarked, 'I didn't realise we were colleagues, I see you've written a book …' The scientific term directs us to a poetry preoccupied with visual perception of the world, and the forensic attention applied simultaneously to the gaze. The blank page is 'like the cornea of an eye' where the poet 'embroider(s)/an iris and in the iris etch(es)/the deep gorge of the retina':

> A gaze then
> sprouts from the page
> and a chasm gapes
> in this yellow notebook.

It's a reflexive poetry, concerned with its own gesture as much as with what it perceives and records. The poems are animated by a careful, precise and logical attentiveness which at the same time recognises that close attention can be a deception. In an early poem not translated by Anthony Molino or Jamie McKendrick, he describes his eyes as pencils which inscribe on the brain indistinct and confused images. Yet paradoxically, if the world is imperfectly grasped, the act of attention is itself a kind of clarification; there is poetry in the myopic gaze:

> *La miopia si fa quindi poesia,*
> *dovendosi avvicinare al mondo*
> *per separarlo dalla luce.*

Anche il tempo subisce questo rallentamento:
I gesti si perdono,
I saluti non vengono colti.
L'unica cosa che si profila nitida
è la prodigiosa difficoltà della visione.

(Myopia makes poetry therefore/having to approach the world/to separate it from the light./Time also endures this slowing down:/gestures are lost, greetings aren't gathered./The only thing which is clear/is the prodigious difficulty of seeing.)

Writing, he reminds us, is not a mirror 'but rather/a shower-screen's frosted glass/– behind which, real enough,/but darkly, a body/is discerned. . .' The rest of that poem points to a paradox where apparent stasis and monotony cohabit with writerly fecundity:

Dieci poesie scritte in un mese
non è molto anche se questa
sarebbe l'undicesima.
Neanche i temi poi sono diversi
anzi c'è un solo tema
ed ha per tema il tema, come adesso.

Ten poems this month
not much, even if this one
does make eleven.
The themes too aren't all that different
in fact, there's only one theme,
the theme itself. Again.
                    (Translated by Anthony Molino)

There's a certain Woody Allenish comedy of the inwardly directed gaze about this, the anxiously self-aware writer with a sense of the absurd yet an equal determination to pursue the apparently small-scale in the knowledge that, in the end, it's the quality of the attention that matters.

Reading a translation, especially a monolingual one like McKendrick's, it can be easy to forget about the relationship the original has with its own tradition and language, but a great deal of Magelli's effect in Italian is the degree to which it's embedded in Italian poetry and relates easily and often playfully with that tradition. A poem like 'A te DNA della poesia' stitches Dante into poetry's DNA as a comic anagram and reminds us the extent to which a contemporary poet's style and resourcefulness are bedded in the

161

tradition of Italian poetry.

The first translations of Magrelli in English to be published in book form were by Anthony Molino, and now he is joined by Jamie McKendrick, whose selection from four books, *The Embrace,* has recently been published by Faber. Molino called his selections from the first two books *Nearsights*, the neologism being an attempt to describe 'the effort to see, to probe, perceive, and communicate the world in a new light.' The effort to see is also the effort to register the seeing, and the result can be 'To write as if/to translate/ something written in another tongue' or, in McKendrick's closer version, 'To write as if this/were a work of translation,/something already penned in another language.' One of the remarkable aspects of the first collection is the primacy it gives to the notebook in which the poems are written, so that it comes to have a life of its own, its existence a statement of intent as well as a constant invitation:

It's not a glass of water that I keep
beside the bed
but this notebook.
Sometimes I sign words there in the dark
and the following day finds them
dumbstruck and battered by the light.
(McKendrick)

It is 'a shield/a trench, a periscope, a loophole.' Like the pen it is a permanent fixture, a constantly alert instrument of apprehension:

The pen should never leave
the hand that writes.
With time it grows into a bone, a finger.
Fingerlike, it scratches, clutches, points.
It's a branch of thought
and yields its own fruits,
offers shelter and shade.
(McKendrick)

This is a long way from Seamus Heaney's pen as spade to dig out the lore and truth of memory. Magrelli's pen is not *like* anything, it is an extension of mind. Part of the reflexiveness of the poems is the transformation of the physical paraphernalia of writing into a world in itself; the page becomes 'a room left unoccupied'. Into this room the poet carries broken chairs or journals, whatever is cast off or 'cashiered from use'. The page or the poem

162

becomes the last refuge of the discarded, 'the last port of call for things/
before sinking beneath the house's horizon/in the clear light of their own
sunset.'

Sometimes it's as if the poet wanted to sail as close to inconsequence as he
can, slowing the world to a stasis where he can subject it to a myopic stare,
almost as if he seeks the doldrums where 'the page lies becalmed', and states
of calm inaction:

> *Domani mattina mi farò una doccia*
> *nient'altro è certo che questo.*
> *Un futuro d'acqua e di talco*
> *in cui non succederà nulla e nessuno*
> *basserà a questa porta. . .*

> I will shower tomorrow morning.
> Besides that, nothing's certain.
> A future of water and talc
> where nothing will happen and no one
> will knock on this door.
>   (Molino)

His second collections *Nature E Venature* (Nature and Veinings) pursues
the same quietist inquisition. One poem imagines the aftermath of gazing:

> *Ho spesso immaginato che gli sguardi*
> *sopravivano all'atto del vedere*
> *come fossero aste,*
> *tragitti misurati, lance*
> *in una battaglia.*
> *Allora penso che dentro una stanza*
> *appena abbandonata*
> *simili tratti debbano restare*
> *qualche tempo sospesi ed incrociati*
> *nell'equilibrio del loro disegno*
> *intatti e sovrapposti come i legni*
> *dello shangai.*

> I've often imagined that looks
> outlive the act of seeing
> as though they were poles
> with measurable trajectories, lances

hurled in a battle.
Then I think that in a room
just left lines
of this kind must stay
for some time poised
criss-cross, cross-hatched,
upholding their structure
like pick-up sticks.
                    (McKendrick)

The poems are a bit like the pick-up sticks left across each other, delicate remnants of an act of inquiry. It's not surprising that the poetry should also proclaim its affection for the discarded, the unimportant, 'all things bust/and putrefied'. Likewise, 'Gestures that go astray/appeal to me...' The human world tends to be kept at a distance, acknowledged through technology that's intimate and distant like the telephone, 'la fontana di voci', 'a shower/where the water never changes/but the drops/differ every time. . .'(Molino). In a typical gesture, one love poem evokes the lover in terms of the digits of her phone number:

The double three,
then the nine that comes third
recall something in your face.
When in search of you
I have to draw up your figure,
I have to spawn the seven ciphers
that are analogues of your name
until the combination safe
of your living voice
unlocks itself.
                    (McKendrick)

The communication itself is haunted by static that 'rucks our voices' and the poet finds himself suspended above the conversation hearing 'the tongue of an ancient creature/from the underworld' calling him. A later poem finds him again haunted by the voices from another room which seem to follow him, making him the soundbox for stories he is not implicated in. This sense of his own removal from the scene is explicitly developed in 'Removals Man' where a metaphor for translation also suggests the relocation of the self.

Magrelli likes to set himself a new challenge with each collection: where the first explores states of stasis and concentration, the second considers more scattered, fragmentary states and the third, *Esercizi di tiptologia* (Typtological Exercises), 1992, is more consciously experimental and includes prose and translations. Typtology, in case we didn't know, is the theory that departed souls communicate with the living by tapping. Maybe the tapping works both ways since the acts of writing and translating might also be seen as communication with the dead. Jamie McKendrick translates a dozen of these poems in *The Embrace*, including the title poem, and they're among the most striking and impressive in the book. The opening poem, a teasing reflection on the inevitable contagion of matter, is a sly triumph:

That matter engenders contagion
if interfered with in its deepest fibres
cut out from its mother like a veal calf
like the pig from its own heart
screaming at the sight of its torn entrails;

That this destruction generates
the same energy that blazes out
when society turns on itself, the temple's veil torn
and the king's head axed from the body of the state
until the faith healer becomes the wound;

That the hearth's embrace is radiation,
nature's pyre, which unravels
helplessly before the smiling company
so as to effect the slightest increase
of the surrounding temperature;

That the form of every production implies
breaking and entry, fission, a final leavetaking,
and that history is the act of combustion
and the Earth a tender stockpile of firewood
left out to dry in the sun,

is hard to credit, is it not?
(McKendrick)

McKendrick doesn't include the prose pieces that are an integral part of *Esercizi di tiptpologia* but they're in Antony Molino's second book of Magrelli translations, *The Contagion of Matter*, and they add greatly to understanding how this poet's imagination works. They have a Ponge-like

165

forensic attention to the object in hand, whether cigarettes, the suburbs of Rome, or his water polo adventures. His water polo piece is dedicated to Nanni Moretti, another enthusiast of the sport, and we might remember that Magrelli makes an appearance as a dermatologist in Moretti's *Caro Diario*, a film whose mordant humour his poetry has much in common with.

One piece considers the plaster casts for Henry Moore's sculptures in a Toronto art museum. The casts seem more convincing, more authentic than the bronze realisations. The spirit of creation lives in the originating material, much as the spirit of poetry might be said to live somewhere in the space between conception and completion.

Some poets gravitate naturally towards, or are animated by the possibilities of an over arching structure. Magrelli's next book, *Didascalie per la lettura di un giornale* (Instructions for reading a newspaper), is a single long poem whose sections correspond to the sections of a newspaper, with titles like 'Date', 'Price', 'Bar Code', 'Review Page', 'Children's Corner'. It is not the individual content of these pages that interests Magrelli, so much as the random arrangement of the world into a set of concerns granted a significance beyond their station by the imprimatur of money and lasting for twenty four hours before their Cinderella-like reversion 'into a pumpkin, expired news,/ money out of circulation, wastepaper.' The most recent book represented in Jamie McKendrick's selection is *Disturbi del sistema binario* (Disruptions of the Binary System). The poems in McKendrick's selection are from the final sequence which derives from Wittgenstein's ambiguous drawing of the 'duckrabbit', which can be seen as a duck or as a rabbit (a hare for Magrelli) and is therefore a figure for the ambiguity with which the world presents itself to us, or with which we perceive it. It allows Magrelli to riff on one of his favourite themes, doubleness or duplicity, and the nature of perception, which have been a constant since *Ora Serrata Retinae*. The last poem here is an apparent leavetaking of language, hinging on the notion that double vision sabotages 'the dream of a shared language' and that what's left is a troubled legacy:

Forked creatures, immune to the word
loomed before me,
and were invulnerable to the truth.
I had entered the age of the duck-hare,
the era of iron, of silence.

Magrelli is clearly determined to renew his work in further, edgier explorations. This might make him seem a schematic writer, but, as McKendrick notes in his introduction, whatever the framework in which each successive book operates, there is a fundamental cohesion in the poems, and an unmistakeable stamp of concerns and personality which comes through the work of both translators. Quizzical, sceptical, mordant, unsettling, playful and deadly serious, the poems seem to issue fitfully, like sudden impulses long incubated, and their force grows in the accumulation, and in the reader's repeated encounter with them. Maybe their success has something to do with their lack of self-satisfaction, the fact that they perpetually acknowledge that their medium is slippery. 'I should like to render in poetry/the equivalent of perspective in painting',

To give a poem the depth of a rabbit
escaping through the fields and make it
distant whilst already
it speeds away from the one who's watching
and veers toward the frame
becoming smaller all the time
and never budging an inch.
The countryside observes
and disposes itself around the creature,
around a point that's vanishing.
                    ('Vanishing Point', translated by Jamie McKendrick)

Tony Roberts

Elaine Feinstein: a very sociable outcast

We are poets, which has the sound of outcast.
Nevertheless, we step out from our shores.
Marina Tsvetaeva

With a prolific writer like Elaine Feinstein it becomes absorbing to watch how, over the course of a great number of books of poetry, she finds her central themes. For me, it was the collection *Badlands* (1986) which heralded her maturity. Hitherto there was as much sorceress as autobiographer to her. This is not to derogate the earlier work, which is most imaginative. Yet from now the more consistently interesting memoirist begins to take over, as friendship develops alongside self and consanguinity as true concerns. *Tout court* she becomes more the traveller in her own relationships, a very sociable outcast.

The *Collected Poems and Translations* (Carcanet, 2002) has a preface with which it might be informative to begin. As Feinstein acknowledges there, people are her central concern; her poems come from her life experiences; she has worked for 'directness and lucidity'. Yet there was an initial complication which has served to colour her vision:

> Part of my resistance to mainstream English poetry of the 1950s, when I first began to write, must lie in my own sense of being an outsider. Born in Liverpool into a family of Jewish immigrants from Odessa, and moreover a woman, it is hardly surprising that three privileged years at Newnham College, Cambridge were not enough to eradicate my sense of being on the periphery.

There were to follow marriage, children, lecturing, editing, journalism, before Feinstein became a full-time writer of poetry (sixteen collections), biography (six), novels (fifteen), radio plays and television dramas. Crucially, Marina Tsvetaeva,

> proved to be the most important single influence on my poetry... She taught me to be unafraid of exposing my least dignified emotions, as well as the technical discipline of a rhythm flowing down a page even when held in stanzas.

In a Green Eye (1966) was Elaine Feinstein's first collection, published when she was thirty six, and characterised by short lines and a strong sense of physical and emotional resilience. If not precocious, the poet is very assured in her delivery. In 'Father', for instance, there is no mistaking the power of diction and image:

> Still boss of his own shop
> he labours in the chippings without grudge
> loading the heavy tables,
> shabby and powerful as an old bus.

The female perspective is not diverted by what was then considered the conventionally feminine. There is nothing tamed here. In 'Calliope in the Labour Ward' the muse is Homeric:

> grunting in gas and air
> they sail to a
> darkness without self
> where no will reaches
>
> in that abandon less
> than human
> give birth
> bleak as a goddess

Neither are we confronted by sentiment in 'Mother Love': 'your shit slides out/yellow and/smelling of curd cheese.' There is a refreshing candour, too, in 'Poor Relations', where she and her cousin 'pity one another' their lot, and then in 'Song of Power':

> For the baiting
> children in my
> son's school class who
> say I am a witch:
> black is the
> mirror you give me

The same engagement is apparent in poems from *Poetry Introduction 1* (1969). In 'Marriage' the voice affirms, 'We have taken our shape from the/damage we do one another'. Again, in 'Against Winter', an old Odessa relative, valued for his 'undisciplined stamina', is presented in his senility and nakedness. Her words on Tsvetaeva come back: *She taught me to be unafraid of exposing my least dignified emotions.*

Having established her mental toughness with that début collection, *The Magic Apple Tree* (1971) has poems 'open to the surprises of the season'. The 'magic' of the title poem is justified, for the poet writes as if bewitched, as in the splendid, 'Anniversary':

> Suppose I took out a slender ketch from
> under the spokes of Palace pier tonight to
> catch a sea going fish for you
>
> or dressed in antique goggles and wings and
> flew down through sycamore leaves into the park

We are all 'supernatural', the poem proclaims *and* we inhabit a supernatural landscape other poems attest:

> angels
> move among us at first light
> over the fields   mysterious
> as April in the grey
> wood of our garden trees.
> ('In the Question of Survival')

Feinstein has always travelled in peopled landscapes. Gardens rather than fields seem to recur. With open land she has more of an academic, naming way. The poet, for all her eagerness to move, is centred by place as she is by relationships. In 'West' we learn: 'new spinach grass or even two/ birds on a black tree/ bind me'. This may be because she is under no illusion: escape is exile to some. Tsvetaeva and Malcolm Lowry are among the casualties, and then there are those she was raised among:

> Estonian ghosts of
> river birds within the
> temples of his skull, ashes
> of poets, girders of school houses:
> these are the tired politics
> that vein his eyes
> ('Exile')

Another theme that has held Feinstein's attention throughout her writing

170

life has been her rôle as a woman, lover and mother. It has many moods of honest self-appraisal. Here we have 'A Prayer for My Sons' which pleads 'Please be free of me' and the romantic:

I carry your lips on my neck
your voice in me, this light,
morning: we can be happy, then,
without presumption
('Happiness')

The Celebrants (1973) is a disturbing collection, relentless in its exploration of the dark side. The title poem deals with the rescue of mystery from the realms of magic. The poet readily acknowledges that harmony – with nature, between lovers, and even within our own bodies – is illusory:

And this knowledge enters even
between the bodies of lovers, though
we share each other's vigil: that our arms

hold water only, salt as the sea
we come from, a spongework of
acid chains, our innermost landscape

an arcane pulp of flexible
chemistry; sinus, tubes,
follicles, cells that wander

Night and water predominate in the collection. 'Night Thoughts' reminds us that 'Nothing can hold forever' and 'Nachtfest' opens,

Water black at night the Rhine and
in small boats lanterns like
coloured souls solemnly passing

into darkness, into circles of silver, into
black quick currents of water hidden as
the trees that rise over us steeply

Nature is not merely metaphor; we are as much its epigones as witnesses. There is little comfort in dreams, in art, in experience. 'A Year Gone' offers the one relief: 'the pain of our questions will melt like the/ wax of our flesh/

into silence.' Yet faith and memory are stubborn. Human tenacity is apparent in 'Love Song' and in 'Survivors', where Feinstein writes of 'the poorest Jews of Rome':

> All that is puzzling to understand
>
> is what the power could be that brings them out
> on Friday night, after so many lessons
> to laugh in garrulous Sabbath on this pavement?

Some Unease and Angels (1977) followed the celebrants with like 'unease'. In 'By the Cam', we read, 'Tonight I think this landscape could/ easily swallow me.' In 'Watersmeet', the poet's perspective is calmed by appreciation of a different contest, that of vegetable and mineral 'kingdoms bonded in hidden warfare underfoot'. Feinstein's mind is habitually on 'the old cold clay soil/and that long, cold kingdom' ('June') and what it buries. In the title poem it is

> as if there
> were messengers asleep in the grass like pollen
> waiting to rise up in sudden flower
>
> angels or darker sentinels, closing in on us

One source of unease is the fear of loss that every person has to live with. It is expressed most clearly at the end of 'Dad':

> I think of you now as once again safely
>   at my mother's side, the earth as
> chosen as a bed, and feel most sorrow for
>   all that was gentle in
> my childhood buried there
>   already forfeit, now forever lost.

Badlands (1986) is the first of Elaine Feinstein's 'journals'. Although the book's blurb speaks of its humour, *Badlands'* dominant note is fortitude. The poet is on the west coast of America; it is that ominous year 1984. Although not autobiographically detailed, the book clearly expresses missing harmony in a key relationship – which might explain the poet's attraction to writing songs for Dido, Penelope and Eurydice in the collection, all women abandoned in one way or another. In 'The Water Magician of San Diego' Feinstein attempts

172

to dent the certainty of a fellow poolside guest, to see him 'waver' in his Californian confidence, whilst acknowledging

– Shall I confess the facts?
I've lived for five years now
as love's hypochondriac, and
it's hard to break the habit.

'A Letter from La Jolla' addresses a former lover. She has recovered from the 'childish spite' of her long ago last letter, she says, and the poem ends with the companionship of dolphins. This does not quite bury the ambiguity with which it opens,

On a balcony in California
being surprised by February
which is the sweet season here, when
blue-scaled grunion dance
on their tails, at high tide
on La Jolla sands, to mate there
and are caught in pails and eaten.

Similarly, 'Home' opens with a question alluding to its title, 'Where is that I wonder?' Another poem recalls Brecht's, 'The man who laughs has not yet heard the appalling news', whereas, in the Cavafy-like 'England', 'the gods are leaving us'. It is of course one thing to be down, another out. There are poems here that celebrate Jean Rhys' spirit and Elizabeth Bishop's 'friendly toughness', and in 'New Year' there is hopeful affirmation:

And as I look back on too many surprises
and face up to next year's uncertainties,
somehow I find it easier and easier
to pray.

City Music (1990) – on the evidence of the *Collected Poems and Translations* – is a collection a little under par. 'Urban Lyric' and 'Convalescence' both suggest recovery from serious illness. Other poems take us back: to childhood, old relatives, old spats. Yet the spirit is bolstered by poetry's strengthening 'our fierce and obstinate centres' ('Muse'), as with the recognition in 'Getting Older' that 'every day won from such/ darkness' is a celebration.

Most moving in its awareness of our insignificance is 'Debts to Marina Tsvetayeva', where Feinstein acknowledges

I have often turned to you in thought as if
your certainties could teach me how to bear
the littleness of what we are on our own
without books, or music, or even a pen;
or as if your stern assurance of the spirit
could preserve us on that ocean we sail alone.

Daylight (1997) is perhaps Elaine Feinstein's most successfully achieved book of poems. A number of poems stand out: 'Homesickness' and 'Rosemary in Provence', for example, for their exquisite sensitivity, and the final 'Prayer', in its open-eyed acceptance. 'Homesickness', a wonderful pen portrait and elegy, begins:

Yesterday I found a postcard with your scrawl:
'Darling, we are all horses, how is it
you haven't learnt that yet?' And at once
your high-boned, white face rose
beside me like a reproach

'Rosemary in Provence' is concerned with the perseverance in age and illness of childlike enthusiasm. It opens:

We stopped the Citroen at the turn of the lane,
because you wanted a sprig of blue rosemary
to take home, and your coat opened awkwardly

Daylight is richly observant in its use of detail. The title reminds us that daylight is both life-giving and illuminating. The senses are particularly acute, attentive to 'the bottleglass blue' of the water off Whale island in 'Picnic' or the air 'heavy with a sweet-smelling citrus' in 'Postcard from the Sporades'. The naming is epicurean. 'Tony' begins:

It was February in Provence and the local market
sold goats' cheese wrapped in chestnut leaves and
thick, painted pottery

and, later, 'you fed us/ beef *daube*, thrush pâté and wine.' A friend's table in 'Homesickness' is 'rich with forest mushrooms, peppers and white cheese'. At Jaffa harbour, 'over Yemenite eggplant and fried dough/ we talk about the Russian exploitation/ of Caesarea two thousand years ago' ('Allegiance'). Atmosphere aside, the intention is to place friends in time, place and conversation – and where better than over food? Several friends are dead. In 'Exile', for Joseph Brodsky (always a magnet to other poets), Feinstein

can remember you talking, as if to yourself,
imagining what it meant to be dead,
with an ironic slant to your face,
and the love of pleasure in your full under-lip
as you nodded up at an untidy bookshelf.
'After that, there is only the book,' you said.

Of course 'God is the wish to live', 'Prayer' reminds us. It is a line that has resonance to this poet steeped in Russian literature, in poetry fierce in its desire to survive amidst turmoil. Clearly the great Russian poets had each other to sustain them, as well as the shades of their predecessors and the shadows of their readers, but Feinstein is rather looking homeward here, as in 'Dead Writers' where she writes, 'Russia treasures her poets, once they're dead./ In England, we depend on one another'. 'Little Venice' explores this last idea, as the poet drives through a neighbourhood that evokes the memory of a friend: 'your words reached through an unhappy/ morning to restore my stamina', it concludes. There are poems here to the old self and to her boys, grown now, but most acute are the poems to friends and companions (many of whom are dedicatees).

Gold (2000) begins with the reminiscences of Lorenzo da Ponte, Mozart's librettist, Jew and priest, bankrupt and criminal, poet and professor. The 'gold' of the title is luck. Da Ponte's colourful life intrigues the reader, though one has to say that it demands so much narrative that Feinstein's long poem rushes along – except for atmospheric moments such as this:

And then it was a tranquil Prague October.
I recall autumn leaves, and birdshell skies;
in an old farmhouse Mozart and Constanze
stayed – I have never heard such birdsong –

More importantly, however, other poems in *Gold* touch on three interrelated themes that are by now central in Feinstein's work: suffering, illness and need. They are autobiographical, but their relevance lies in their universality. Love is seen as debilitating as well as sublime. In fact, at times, her poems read like notes from a needy friend:

How can we make friends before one of us dies
if you quarrel with two fingers in your ears,

175

like a child? Things won't come out right now.
You think I don't love you. I won't argue.
Your angry sadness stings me into tears.

.   ('Living Room')

'Casualty' deals with illness, hope and the common regret, 'What/ a mistake
to let an ambulance/ carry me off to this wretched ward.' 'Prayer for my Son'
speaks for itself. 'Respite' recounts the way things are now:

Rain in the beech trees at 4 a.m.:
I ran away from your voice to
sit in an upright chair. Useless
in your despair, I had no
strength to scoop you
out of your long story,
let alone think of rescue.

'Options' flirts with the way they might have been, as the poet returns to
considering a relationship in her past:

Illicit one-time love, your face
was narrow as mine, Italian as
De Niro. You were fortunate
to escape marriage to me, yet
sometimes, I confess, you visit
my salacious dreams.

In Feinstein's autobiographical poems – *if* the voice and poet are one
– she sometimes seems to stack the odds against marital harmony with
such confessions. A more oblique approach is found in 'Jeopardy', which
sublimates rejection with its Odyssean twist, with Calypso 'Relishing
the energy of his self-concern,/ you have already forgiven his onward
journey.'

Those lines have an unexpected finality, since Elaine Feinstein lost her
husband before *Talking to the Dead* (2007), which deals with the subject of
their long and – by the witness of the poems – occasionally difficult marriage.
This collection recalls the intimacies and ambivalence of a marriage in which
we frequently hear the husband's voice. The book begins with 'Winter' and
ends with 'London', a poem to her eight year old granddaughter. (As with
several of her poems to children and grandchildren, it begins in delight and
ends in prayer.) Yet it was 'Winter' which shocked me when I first opened

the collection in a book shop at the time of its publication. The poet warns us that her thoughts are 'bleak'. The first five lines cannot rescue us from the frightening, impotent image that ends the poem:

You never did learn to talk and find the way
at the same time, your voice teases me.
Well, you're right, I've missed my turning,
and smile a moment at the memory

always knowing you lie peaceful and curled
like an embryo under the squelchy ground,
without a birth to wait for, whirled
into that darkness where nothing is found.

Nevertheless, what might be a book of despair turns into a celebration of recollection:

I still remember love like another country
with an almost forgotten landscape
of salty skin and a dry mouth.
('A Visit')

Indeed, the success achieved in *Talking to the Dead* is in the poet's evoking, through memory, her late husband's presence:

You had big hands, strong hands, gentle
as those of a Mediterranean father
caressing the head of a child.

    Hold my hand, you said. *I feel*
    I won't die while you are here
('Hands')

Elaine Feinstein's latest book of poems, *Cities* (2010), illustrates that there is life after a death, albeit much of it is remembered. The collection is a trawl through travels, a number of which were hampered by political repression. Her point of entrance in this collection is a sympathy, a racial sensitivity, to suffering and diaspora. 'Migrations', the opening poem, begins with the celestial navigation of birds to our shores, 'avian immigration' as the poet has it. Survival is allusion's bridge here, for immigrants arrive also:

holding fast to old religions
and histories, remembering
the shock of being hunted in the streets,
the pain at leaving their dead
in broken cemeteries, their resilience
hardwired as birds' skill in navigation.

The poet's hope is for 'migration, symbiosis, assimilation'. Having family roots in Odessa a century back, she wants 'to make common cause with them.' The words 'remember' and 'memory' echo throughout *Cities*. It is a historical and geographical journal: of friends and family and of a younger self in late forties Cambridge, learning about love and 'the first salt lick of poetry' ('Portugal Place, Cambridge'). These memories are inevitably bitter-sweet. 'Loss' speaks of the distress of an old friendship cooling. 'Christmas Day in Willesden Green' evokes the pride and pain in the company of an autistic grandchild and 'Rush Cutter Bay, Sydney' offers pain and yet that characteristic fortitude:

How could I guess
the pain waiting on the next page for me?
The blank of betrayal which would
rapidly scoop out my life and release
the blood flow of poetry

The absence of self-pity in Feinstein drives the poetry. Given the bloody history of the last century and the geography of her travels, however, there is an air of menace to *Cities*. Familial and ethnic suffering has sharpened her natural sensitivity. As she acknowledges in 'A Weekend in Berlin, 2008':

Only at the Hotel Adler, when
a flunkey shakes his head
do I have a shiver of unease as if
encountering the dead.

The literary has always offered a context in Feinstein's poetry. So 'Warsaw, 1973' opens cinematically in:

Wajda's city of ashes and diamonds, where
a fairground wheel once turned
to carnival music while the ghetto burned.

The poems are also deft in their characterisation. In 'Lublin, 1973' Czeslaw Milosz is called upon to explain how '*The Polish accent sticks to the palate/ across three languages.*' Sitting at a table with that irrepressible raconteur, in 'Isaiah Berlin in Rome', Feinstein remembers Virginia Woolf 'once/described him with unkind surprise:/ *a swarthy Portuguese Jew – until he speaks.*' Feinstein has always been an insatiable story teller herself and in 'Budapest' captures both the city and the likeness of the poet, Janos Pilinszky:

his parchment face is bloodless,
lit like a lamp from within,
his bones fine, his lips
shrewdly curved, humorous.

Cities is a highly rewarding collection and, to me, it is the poetry of the last thirteen years – 'Daylight', 'Gold', 'Talking to the Dead' and 'Cities' – which has explored Elaine Feinstein's life and heritage most successfully. Always in her sociable restlessness I hear Tsvetaeva's lines from 'I know the truth':

The wind is level now, the earth is wet with dew,
the storm of stars in the sky will turn to quiet.
And soon all of us will sleep under the earth, we
who never let each other sleep above it.

Douglas Houston

Dusk

Night's already seeping from the screen
Of boughs and briars the fence can't contain
At the western end of the pub car park,
Where the kids can practise swearing undisturbed
And nothing marks where the loser died
In a fight that happened before they were born.

Later, they're down by the canal,
Water spurting aerated jets
Through cracks in the black lock gates.
Somebody's drunken uncle drowned here
The last time he took the short-cut home.

You have watched the generations inherit
Their patterns of years in the weave of this place
Where your own threads run their bright strands.
Dear woman, hold my hand, please, while the sun
Is setting on all this living and dying
Brought hot to the anvil of days.

Beside Still Waters

Where the canal opens its long view
Down the level furlongs, one bank
Is steep, impenetrably overhung
With arboreal generations competing
For space to grow new boughs they spread above
The briars entangling crumbled brickwork
And patches of abandoned workshop floors.

The other bank is paved, has bordering trees
Wild and abundant with filberts and cherries,
Black and red, that nobody picks but us.
You were there, girl-child of the secret places
Where we lived for hours on nuts and berries,
Where our Dads and school could never find us,
And what we found and hid is always waiting.

Ian Parks

Optimism in the Night

Douglas Houston: *Beyond the Playing Fields: New and Selected Poems 1980-2010* (Shoestring Press, £12.00)

I'd like to begin, perversely, with a poem which is inexplicably absent from this *Selected*: the wonderful and enigmatic 'The Return' which was the first poem by Douglas Houston I read. I found it in the pages of the *A Rumoured City* anthology which brought together poets associated with the city and university of Hull. It subsequently appeared in Houston's first collection, *With the Offal Eaters* and is short enough to quote in full:

> The poet led me out among the quays
> Where light discloses luminous desires,
> Like neon leeches twitching their small fires
> In cisterns of original disease.
>
> There was no speaking in that dismal peace;
> Looks asked and answered all there was to know.
> The air was static as the vaulted stone
> That fixed the limits where all sequence ceased.
>
> My guide politely nodded his *adieu*,
> Then, stepping into shadow, disappeared.
> Escape was not as hard as I had feared;
> I followed clues of light that filtered through
>
> A dim expanse of culverts and canals.
> I first saw day through grilles, then over walls;
> Paved banks gave way to grass where waterfalls
> Accompanied the birds in spring chorales.

It's all there: the exemplary control of form, the slight sense of menace and unease, the reserved yet intimate address to the reader, the faultless precision of the language, the sense that the poem is 'about' something, the deference to past masters and the extraordinary vividness of the images employed – all of which have marked Houston's subsequent work and made it singular. Houston is not a poet of the moment; his work reflects on ideas and intense moments of epiphany but does so in a controlled manner so that 'emotion recollected in tranquillity' (to borrow Wordsworth's phrase) is the informing principle behind his achievement. And the publication of this *Selected* provides us with ample evidence of just how considerable that achievement is.

As it is, Houston's *Selected* opens with one of his finest and most definitive poems, 'Devotions' where the speaker

> Having mortified myself with a hangover
> Deliberately conceived on two days' hard drinking

finds himself

> standing underneath the end of the pier
> In the year's high ritual of my seagull worship,
> Which demands such unbreakfasted, humbling rigours
> And will culminate with prostration in the surf
> After the solemn dispensation of breadcrusts.

The line between the real and surreal is finely drawn. Houston's poems invariably take place in a recognisable locale but are distinguished by their flights of fancy and their enviable facility for investing the mundane with the extraordinary. His definition of worship here as 'a proper respect got out of hand' reminds us of the poet's debt to Auden whose example casts a long shadow over this *Selected*. Auden is to Houston what Horace was to Auden – a presiding spirit. However much of a presence Auden is – either explicitly as in 'W. H. Auden in Cwmbrwyno' or as a point of reference in the more 'public' poems – Houston is always his own man, learning and responding to Auden in an ongoing dialogue rather than merely imitating him. Other influences include the Augustan poets, and Houston's unmistakable gift for satire is filtered through a lyric sensibility of the first order. And it is tempered with humour. Take, for instance, 'Lines on a Van's Dereliction' where the high style we might associate with the poetry of Dryden and Pope is employed to great effect:

> This rust-infested cage with worn-out breaks,
> Green paintwork scratched as if a demon'd clawed it,
> Calls forth these tribute lines for old time's sake –
> Its future's scrap, I simply can't afford it.

The poem goes on to list the speaker's intimate connection with the van through a series of adventures and misadventures and concludes memorably with:

Infinity's before us right from birth;
So don't take it too badly rusty friend,
Should I dismember you to sell as parts.
Remember being doesn't simply end:
Disintegration's where the big time starts.

I can think of no other poet writing today who could pull this off with such confidence, flare and conviction. It's partly a matter of the register and tone; partly the sheer joy of seeing the technical facility at work; partly the wit and playfulness of a poet writing at the height of his powers. Humour too is present in Houston's second collection, *The Hunters in the Snow* which was published in 1995. 'Poet Laureate Ritual Bath Murder' vividly imagines none other than Ted Hughes lurking 'outside the bathroom door':

When your head goes under the water
To rinse away the shampoo,
That's Ted, that cold on your dripping back,
And he knows what he's got to do.

The final stanza relishes the fact that it is as menacing as it is hilarious:

The bath's gone cold as he gets out
The curving silver knife
And when he's done he'll go downstairs
And do things with your wife.

But it isn't all laughs. Houston has written heartbreaking elegies for his father, dense and prophetic poems about the imminent onslaught of a nuclear winter, and love poems that are subtle, musical and deeply felt.

As far back as 1982, when Douglas Dunn was addressing Houston's work in his introduction to *A Rumoured City,* he drew attention to the fact that the poems were 'unashamedly literary' effecting a delicate 'balance between the erudite and the colloquial'. Much of what Dunn said back then still holds, although Houston has developed his range and technique in a career that now spans over three decades. Apart from featuring generous selections from all of Houston's previous collections (including the remarkable *The Welsh Book of the Dead*), this collection also includes many uncollected poems from 1980-2010. Of these, 'To Lavernock Point' is most representative and a thing of beauty. And beauty arises as much from the sound of these poems as from the sense. In an illuminating interview with Stephen Smith in *Bête Noire,* Houston stated that 'I'm not a dogmatic proponent of the technically traditional approach but for me it provides a basis. Villanelles and sonnets abound in this *Selected* but the form never draws attention to itself to the detriment of the poem; Houston always uses it as a vehicle for the melding of sound and sense.

My only criticism of *Beyond the Playing Fields* is that it is too slim. Apart from the omission of 'The Return', there are many individual poems that have slipped through the net. Where, for instance, is 'Driver' – one of Houston's finest and most idiosyncratic lyrics?

> My headlights dust moths out past the town,
> And cruising at sixty miles an hour I think of you,
> Sweeter than all the chocolate on the road.'

I'm fully aware that a *Selected Poems* is just that – the poet choosing the best and most representative of their poems to make some sort of statement about what they've been trying to do. We have to wait, unfortunately, for a collected before we see some of these fine poems in print again. Houston has a distinctive and fully developed voice. For those coming to his work for the first time this *Selected* is highly recommended, and a good place to start would be with individual poems like 'Day in, Day Out' ('I look for optimism in the night / While urinating onto the dark earth'), 'Slate City', 'Huddersfield 2010' and 'School' (a line of which provides the subtitle for the collection). Underlying the wit and the technical brilliance, the playfulness and conversational tone, there lies a poet of great power and originality, not afraid to acknowledge his influences or to take on the big questions that beset us all. What more could we ask of a poet?

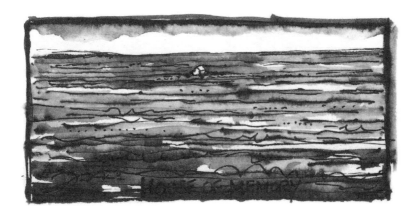

Annemarie Ní Churreáin, 29, is originally from Donegal,
but now lives in Dublin. She is a native Irish speaker with a degree in
Communication Studies from DCU, and an M.Phil in Creative Writing from
the Oscar Wilde Centre at Trinity College, Dublin. At the moment she is
employed by the Irish Association of Creative Arts Therapists. Her poems
have appeared in *The Stinging Fly, Poetry Ireland Review* and *The Shop*. She
has also been published in a recent anthology, *Leave Us Some Unreality*. Her
poems in English are influenced by her native language, Irish.

The Lane

Breathless, the whole way
down, skimming
fuchsia, rag-ferns,

to the road below
where an old school bus
waited;

a stream of girls,
wet hair trailing
a scent of apples

in the left-behind air,
orchards
imagined us

fetching from wells,
pitchers of silver equations,
poems, plant names.

In the evenings,
pale foreheads throbbed,
small steps

returning uphill
fell
into careless unison,

something
on those short journeys
between worlds

conjured
sisterhood
from unshared histories,

separate blood,
incomparable desires
after summer

when the lane
was high with new grass
and each girl

had her own dream
to swim
in the greenness.

End of Girlhood

The first time
a tree called me by name,
I was thirteen and only spoke a weave of ordinary tongues.

It started with a leaf and next,
a mist came down from the hills, beating a lone skin drum,
looking for me.

Scarlet pimpernels dropped hints
that could not be ignored:
no red is innocent.

Badger trails called me aside for a word.
Come underground, they said,
see what we are made of.

Safe House

It is said, there was a child
whose name shimmered on tongues,
sounding foreign,

going from home to home
with only a torn voice
calling sometimes

to read stories
until no new coins dropped
and the line went still.

At night, the child climbed
cot rails, tumbled out
over edges,

white as a slapped bag of flour,
becoming the hours
she sat through,

knowing already
that what kept her awake
could not end in dreams.

The Milk-Run

There were nights
when my father whispered me awake
and still part asleep, I'd rise into clothes,
float towards a corridor's end.

All along back roads
in a pick-up truck beneath the moon,
we left cartons on doorsteps,
ticked names off lists,
humoured dogs.

Two sisters, who lived
in a house with flagstone tiles,
burned a light all night behind an open door.
No power had reached there yet.
Under a tyre's grind, dirt gravel
rose through notes of diesel and souring milk
as dawn half-broke
over Errigal.

Tibetan Sweetbread

Word travels all over
like a blackish smoke,
choking hill-roads:

two men dead in last night's rain,
struggling with dirt veins
and monsoon mud.

Plastic wind-sheets
shudder in the empty streets
when I pass through unseen,

arriving alone to class,
where my teacher kneels
beside a straw mat for a table,

a single hot-plate,
and all the spare ingredients
that could be gathered today

in a closed village,
the making of bread
begins,

let this bread be our language,
flour is the first word,
water drops bind,

knead, waste not,
scour the bowl's inside,
patiently we work.

Out of last, palm slaps
a white cloud forms
I press my hand

upon the flat pastry,
make it smooth
as the word 'mourn'.

Richie McCaffery is 24 and lives in Stirling. He works as a trainee youth worker in Callander and is applying to do a Ph.D at Glasgow University on the Scottish Poetry of World War Two. His poems have been accepted by, among other journals, *Stand, Magma, Envoi, Iota, Other Poetry, Poetry Salzburg Review.* He is compiling his first pamphlet of poems for publication, possibly in 2012, by HappenStance Press.

Busker

Port Street, Stirling

For every string
he has snapped
along the way,

on his battered
Eko acoustic,
he sings deeper.

The inner city
cold is marmoreal,
the barked breath

of his song.
Each word
passed down

from the masters,
made his own
through his mistakes

is an instant
ghost
before him.

Going Straight

He's going straight he tells her.
It's early evening and all the pints
are footloose, not yet car crashes.

He's really changed, he insists.
He's broken rocks in the hot sun
and found ammonite after ammonite

wrapped up in its own importance.
He will straighten them out, unravel
their mineral chicanes, their bent ways.

He just needs another chance to prove
himself. Forgiveness is almost his drug
the way he begs for another hit of it.

Rings

You drip your rings
into a Moorish box
every night and take
a quick inventory
should they vanish.

Your grandmother's
opal, the one of bone
the other blue glass.
Your engagement ring
like waves at Orkney

I often wonder what
you must dream about,
for you to denude
your fingers like that.
As the rings lie there

in velvet lined night.
Do they keep tight
the silver gold grip
around the circular air
of your promises?

Woodwork

I have smoked a whole day down to the stub
working in wood. First I cleared a dying room
of furniture, mostly repro-regency stuff
that I blitzed in the garden with a hammer.

Cupboards fell away like jerry-built coffins.
There was a sprained ash, its roots poisoned
by one of my mother's neighbourly feuds.
I chainsawed its thirty year concentric archive

down to little logs. A friend came over, invited
me for a pint, he asked was there any need
to cut everything up so small? Then it dawned
on me what I'd been doing and I told him

everyman's history is so crammed with important
things beyond the sceptred days of nationhood
that a jaundiced tree, or my mother's dressing table,
will segue into yesterday only in hideable bits.

40 Watt Bulb

He was just a tungsten cilium
away from Homeric darkness.

He practised for many moons
with his autumnal hair to thread

light through the eye of a needle
so he could once more sew the sun

back from where it fell that day,
like a lapsarian apple that lies

on the grass, its cidering flesh
only half longing for the bough.

NOTES FOR BROADSHEET POETS

Aviva Dautch was born in Salford in 1978 and now lives in London where she works as a Creative Educator for The British Library. She began writing seriously just over four years ago and her first published poems appeared in *Agenda*'s Broadsheet 10. Since then publications include *Modern Poetry in Translation, The Long Poem Magazine* and *Poetry Review*, for whom she regularly reviews. In 2010 she graduated with Distinction from the MA in Creative Writing at Goldsmiths and received the Faber Academy's Faber & Faber Fellowship. In Summer 2011 she has articles forthcoming in *Poetry Review* and *The Jewish Quarterly* and poems in a poetry edition of *Twin* curated by Jo Shapcott.

In the following essay, 'Like A Summer Of Locusts', Aviva explains how reading John Burnside's *Gift Songs* led her to write her own long poem 'Grasshoppers' (printed in this issue). When I asked Aviva how she first came to writing poetry, 'reading' was key:

My family was Jewish and quite religious so I grew up with the rhythms of Hebrew liturgy. In English, the only place to find that intensity of language and sound was in poetry. I read Shakespeare and the Metaphysicals, then discovered contemporary poetry in my early twenties. It took several years of reading before I had the courage and the knowledge to begin to write properly but when I started writing I was very lucky to find great mentors early on. I studied 'Versification' with Mimi Khalvati, who has continued to encourage and advise me. The other really significant meeting was with Fiona Sampson, who gave me an internship at Poetry Review. *For a year, I worked with Fiona for a day a week, learning from her acute eye and thoughtful editing. Mimi's and Fiona's warmth and generosity has been very important, as has that of my teachers on the MA and at the Faber Academy, but equally necessary has been the relationship with poets I only know on the page. Reading work I've loved, and using it as inspiration to experiment with different techniques, has helped me widen my ambition for my writing. Holding up my own first attempts against the work of people I admire, such as John Burnside, is a risky thing to do – especially since all I see is what's still to be achieved, but perhaps dissatisfaction is a good thing… it's certainly the most powerful motivating force to drive continuing work.*

Like A Summer Of Locusts: On Reading John Burnside's *Gift Songs*

Despite my literary critical 'death of the author' training, I order John Burnside's memoirs off Amazon. First *A Lie About My Father*, then *Waking*

Up In Toytown arrive, and I learn about a foundling father, alcoholism and violence, mental illness and dreams of Surbiton, the landscapes and bodies that people his life. What I don't find is John Burnside, The Poet. His prose has the same sinuous magic as his song yet is a different creature since, like the 'God of St Paul' Burnside is drawn to, the God of Poetry is 'no respecter of persons'. I've never met John Burnside in person. And despite some shared resonances – religious upbringings, experiences of violence, childhoods slipping on shifting truths – it isn't our histories or the acts we perform in our everyday lives that pulls me to his poetry. I relate to him not biographically, person-to-person, but in a more immediate, intimate way, for his poems aren't about a performed 'personhood' but a reaching for 'self': 'the self / that loves what it will / and watches us quicken and fade / with the passing of time'. I am drawn to 'its deftness, on nights like this, / its immutable grace' ('Ama Et Fac Quod Vis').

Reading as a writer can be a carnivorous activity. Good poems have a fizzing energy to them: like locusts voraciously consuming crops we read for the electric charge, devour it to power our own writing. I know this sounds selfish – as if writerly reading is a purely self-serving act – but it feels the very opposite: a tactile and generous relationship. This seems particularly true when reading Burnside's *Gift Songs* (Cape: 2007), the title a nod to the Shakers whose test of a song's goodness was how much of a gift it was. He presents the poems to the reader like wine and communion wafer, so that in the mouth they'll mutate into blood, into flesh. This is religion as realignment: the book deconstructs the etymology of *re-ligere* as meaning 'renewal of connection', and I find the 'gracile revelation' of 'De Corporis Resurrectione' an intensely physical one; both his language and my own epidermis simultaneously becoming more transparent, the reading itself a process of osmosis, 'leaching away through the glass / like remembered skin.'

Transubstantiation is central to Burnside's poetics for, while intellect is visceral, he sees the body as metaphor:

as if it had long been decided
that flesh is a journey,
something immense in the blood,
like a summer of locusts,

or something not quite visible, but quick
as birchseed, or the threading of a wire
through sleep and rapture, gathering the hand
that reaches from the light, to close, or open.'
('For A Free Church')

Burnside's hand is constantly outstretched, open to the reader but also receiving 'always the gift of the world'. The corporeal is an elastic concept, extending past his own physicality to the creaturely and, beyond that, to the corpus of Christian text, before finally reaching towards the horizon: 'the scent of beasts arrives;/ the biblical;// rudderless gazes/ turned to a farmer's sky.' Throughout this sequence the stanzas are elegant, the language tightly condensed, but the mind behind them is expansive.

That Burnside's poetry demands a multi-dimensional reading seems obvious from the generosity with which he reads others. In a recent essay, 'Dreaming A Buffalo' (*Poetry Review* 100:3), he uses Lucie Brock-Broido's 'Self-Portrait On The Grassy Knoll' as a call to think in technicolor and possess more than 'a black and white picture of the world'. He sees the yellow of Brock-Broido's 'mustardseed' as not just 'a genetically modified crop'; it's the 'vivid colour and fuzziness of the lived experience' and 'invokes Matthew 13:31 – "the kingdom of heaven is like to a grain of mustard seed which a man took and sowed in his field"'. In Burnside's reading of Brock-Broido's lines, the tiniest of plants booms with resonance along both horizontal and vertical axes: encompassing time and depth; the personal and the mythic. In the same way, his own poetry requires us to find the world in 'the nothing at my shoulder', a space which is simultaneously 'miracle' and 'utter void' ('Ny-Hellesund').

Burnside seems to be constantly reaching for the intangible, searching for the numinous in lack and absences: 'the gap between darkness and light has already vanished/ […] all that remains […] / is the scent on his skin, a scent he mistakes for the spirit.' In 'Notes Towards A Supreme Fiction', Wallace Stevens suggests 'not to have is the beginning of desire'. In Burnside's universe it seems fiction and faith are inextricably linked, and desire becomes a driving force. One of the epigraphs to the collection is a quotation from another American poet, Rodney Jones: 'Fiction's inside like faith. / It doesn't count unless you believe it, and / you don't have to know it for it to be the truth.' There are inner truths here, in invisible spaces, but for John Burnside they are located and framed by the body, 'and what the body offers of itself'. His other epigraph is Genesis 32:29, when Jacob asks the Angel to 'Tell me, I pray thee, thy name.' Jacob's search to pin down divinity results in a different naming as his own is changed to 'Israel' – one who wrestles with God. The philosophical exchange is located in a corporeal one; this episode happens after the Angel has prevented Jacob from continuing along his path, and in response Jacob and the Angel have physically fought, swopping blow after blow.

For Burnside, the body is essential as a frame for 'any journey, any secret thing / that passes in the dark and flits away: / not self, but history; not self, but place'. History and place can be found in other bodies as well as the human one, in 'chapel and harbour and hearth' and also 'in everything in between: the sea and sky' ('Le Croisic'). These liminal spaces are the ones I'm drawn to; I inhabit them alongside Burnside, 'till all the dreams we had / were dreams of water' ('By Pittenweem'). Burnside's gifts of song – of dreams, water and the body – acknowledge the subjective nature of our distinct experiences as individuals, but reach beyond that, attempting to touch another consciousness while holding in tension an awareness that the attempt is both creating a fiction and containing deeper truth. I read his *Gift Songs* and write one of my own: 'Grasshoppers'. It is drawn from my distinct experience: I am a woman, and one writing out of a Jewish not a Christian tradition; my lands are neither Scotland or America, but England and Israel; the liquid that holds my dreams has a more limited reach – bathwater rather than 'the firth'. If, like Burnside, I see 'the body as metaphor', my body is a contested and occupied space with shifting boundaries. Yet despite our differences, there's a freedom he gives me: to allow the personal, the infinitesimally small, to hold big political questions. And what I learn from him about craft is that it's important to frame the metaphysical, the existential, within a carefully controlled form. When I try out his stepped lines, suddenly there's a vertical drive down the page… an openness blows into my poem, thoughts spin out radially rather than following their usual, linear, path. I am unsure how to handle this and turn back to Burnside's work, to trace his subtle perceptual negotiations and learn by mimesis.

'Saint Nazaire', the first of his Eliot-inspired 'Four Quartets', opens with plane leaves drifting around the Catholic church, 'freeze-dried, silent, wrapping-paper brown'. Burnside begins with the thingy-ness of things, locating his ideas in closely observed concrete details in a way that would satisfy even William Carlos Williams. The leaves take us to the landscape: 'they gather in the nooks between abandoned / hair salons and shuttered pharmacies, or swirl around in broken alleyways / till everything is powder'. Suddenly the natural is jammed up against the urban, the whole lot disintegrating, 'leaves and stalks / and sand-drift, all / *in pulverem*'. And with the Latin phrase we immediately shift register: the powder transforms into the dust of death; walking alongside us through the 'windless innertown', with its 'breeze-blocks, mongrels, smashed glass' is the Psalmist, calling out supplications on behalf of the poor. Yet not everything is pulverised, what stays intact are 'the rock-cress in the kerbstones and the char-black /ganglia of fallen Judas pods'. I look up the meaning of 'ganglia' – synonymous with 'clusters' in computer-speak, it leads me to imagine bundles of black wires, plant-life taking on the hardness of a plastic artifice. What has 'fallen' (even the verb returns us to the Bible) are seed pods from the 'Honesty'

197

plant, known for having the appearance of coins – the allusion is to Judas Iscariot and his thirty pieces of silver. Money for betrayal: a body of wealth gained, a betrayed human body wracked with the pain of a tortuous death. So now I'm back to 'ganglia', used anatomically for a mass of nerve cells, and my own nerves are jangling at the sheer guts of the man! For here is an instant, painful, political comment on our modern consumerist society and the inequality of suffering it has produced, through an intricate and finely-tuned network of religious reference and description of place. Burnside's gaze is that of an insect's multi-faceted eye, each surface refracting light along a slightly different dimension, building up a far richer vision than that perceived by my own convex lens.

Burnside isn't afraid to challenge his readers, to trust us to follow his diversifying threads, allowing us to go outwards from the poem by following his exegesis of Biblical texts, then drawing us back in, forcing us to read ourselves into the worlds he's creating and to parallel his eisegesis with our own. This is the very opposite of ambiguity; permitting his poems this kind of mystery requires utter precision of language. In search of an equally accurate music, I edit my writing over and over again, but find I'm living with constant dissatisfaction. I begin to acknowledge that this is not just caused by my inability to fully realise Coleridge's requirement of 'the best words in the best order' but a longing for, and fear of, the revelatory contact of opening my 'self' to others. There is white space here for the readers to read themselves into, but what will they – you – make of it? I am comparatively new to this kind of writing and suddenly its demands seem absurd, its rewards painfully uncertain. This is poetry as extreme risk. So, for perhaps the first time, I go back to John Burnside not for challenge, but for reassurance that it's worth it, take comfort in his 'rule of the tundra':

> the logic of the wilderness that says
> where nothing seems to happen
> all the time
> what happens is the chance
> that something might.
>
> ('Five Animals')

Biographies

Gary Allen was born in Ballymena, Co. Antrim. He has been published widely in magazines, including *Agenda*, *Ambit*, *The Dark Horse*, *Edinburgh Review*, *Irish Pages*, *London Magazine*, *Poetry Ireland*, *The Poetry Review*, *Stand* etc. He has published ten collections of poetry including *Iscariot's Dream*, by *Agenda* Editions (2008). His latest collection is *The Next Room*, by Lapwing Press. A new collection, *Ha, Ha*, is due this year from Lagan Press. A selection of his poems has just been published in the anthology, *The New North*, re-published by Salt.

Josephine Balmer's latest collection, *The Word for Sorrow*, was published by Salt in 2009. Previous collections and translations include *Chasing Catullus: Poems, Translations and Transgressions*, *Catullus: Poems of Love and Hate*, *Classical Women Poets* and *Sappho: Poems & Fragments*, all Bloodaxe. She is presently working on a study of her work as a poet/translator for Oxford University Press's 'Classical Presences' series.

David Borthwick teaches literature at the University of Glasgow's School of Interdisciplinary Studies, based in Dumfries, South West Scotland (www.glasgow. ac.uk/dumfries). He specialises in modern and contemporary Scottish literature and has published on John Burnside, Lewis Grassic Gibbon, A.L. Kennedy and Irvine Welsh. Increasingly, his research concerns literature's responses to historical and contemporary environmental conditions, in particular poetic responses to landscape and place. He is currently writing a monograph on John Burnside.

Zoë Brigley is originally from South Wales. Her first poetry collection, *The Secret* (Bloodaxe 2007), was a Poetry Book Society Recommendation and was long-listed for the international Dylan Thomas Prize. Her writing has appeared in publications like *Calyx*, *The Manhattan Review*, *The Times Higher Education* and *PN Review*. She writes a blog *The Midnight Heart*, and she edited *Feminism, Literature and Rape Narratives* (Routledge 2010). She currently lives in Pennsylvania, USA.

Andy Brown's most recent publications are *Goose Music* (with John Burnside, Salt), *Fall of the Rebel Angels: poems 1996-2006* (Salt), and *The Storm Berm* (Tall Lighthouse). He is Director of Creative Writing at the University of Exeter, and was formerly a Centre Director for the Arvon Foundation at Totleigh Barton. He studied ecology, which informs both his poetry and his critical writing. He is a regular tutor for the Poetry School and for Arvon, and is currently working on a book of poems based on the paintings of Hieronymus Bosch.

Louise C. Callaghan was born in 1948 and was brought up in County Dublin, Ireland. She lives in Dublin. Her latest poetry collection *In The Ninth House* was published by Salmon Poetry in 2010. Her previous poetry collections are *The Puzzle-Heart* (Salmon, 1999) and *Remember the Birds* (Salmon, 2005). Her poetry is widely anthologised in Ireland and England. She completed an M.Litt in Creative Writing at St. Andrews University in 2007, receiving a First Class Honours in her poetry dissertation.

Christopher Crawford was born in Glasgow, Scotland. His poems, fiction and translations have most recently appeared or are forthcoming in *Rattle, Orbis, Envoi, The Cortland Review, Eyewear, Now Culture* and the anthology *The Return of Kral Majales: Prague's Literary Renaissance 1990-2010*.

Peter Dale's most recent publications are *Peter Dale in Conversation with Cynthia Haven*, published by Between the Lines Press, *Under the Breath*, poems, and *Wry-Blue Loves,* a verse translation of Tristan Corbière, which received a Poetry Book Society Recommendation for Translation – both published by Anvil Press Poetry, as is his terza rima translation of *The Divine Comedy*, now going into its seventh edition. His translation of Paul Valéry, *Charms and Other Pieces*, Anvil, appeared in 2007 and is now in its second edition. His current book of verse is the sequence *Local Habitation*, 2009, also from Anvil who will publish his new book, *Diffractions: New and Collected Poems* in 2011. He now lives in Cardiff.

Gemma Green, 38, studied Classics at university and gained an MA in Creative Writing at the University of East Anglia under the guidance of Andrew Motion. Her poetry has appeared in magazines and anthologies and in 2008 she won 2nd prize in the *Daily Telegraph* Poetry for Performance competition and has since been shortlisted for the Bridport Prize, *Mslexia* Poetry Competition, the Tall Lighthouse Pamphlet competition and won 3rd prize in the Essex International Poetry competition. In 2010 Gemma was selected by the Arvon Foundation for their Jerwood Mentoring scheme and has spent the last year being mentored by Jo Shapcott.

Harry Guest was born in Penarth in 1932. He lives in Exeter. He read Modern Languages at Cambridge and taught in schools and universities in France, Japan and the UK before retiring in 1991.His Collected Poems, *A Puzzling Harvest*, appeared from Anvil in 2002. Since 1994 he has been an Honorary Research Fellow of the University of Exeter. In 1998 he was awarded an Honorary Doctorate of Letters by the University of Plymouth. He was elected to The Welsh Academy in 2001. His latest collection is *Some Times* (Anvil, 2010).

Chris Hardy's poems have appeared in *the Rialto, Poetry Review, the North, Tears in the Fence, Acumen*, poetrypf.co.uk, nthposition.com and many other places. He has won prizes in the National Poetry Society's and other competitions. One poem was in the 2009 Forward Prize Anthology and four in the new Eland anthology, *The Isles Of Greece*. Two collections of his poetry have been published: *Swimming In The Deep Diamond Mine* (Hub) and *A Moment Of Attention* (Original Plus).

Eleanor Hooker has been selected for the Poetry Ireland *Introductions Series 201*. She has recently been awarded an MPhil in Creative Writing, with Distinction, from Trinity College, Dublin. Eleanor has had poems published in: *Crannog, The Stinging Fly* and *The SHOp* and in *Leave Us Some Unreality*, an anthology of new writing from the Oscar Wilde Centre, Trinity College Dublin. She began her career as a nurse and midwife. She has a BA (Hons 1st) from the Open University and an MA (Hons) in Cultural History from the University of Northumbria. She is founding member and Vice-Chairperson of the Dromineer Literary Festival in Ireland. She is a helm and Press Officer for the Lough Derg RNLI Lifeboat.

Douglas Houston was born in Cardiff in 1947 and grew up in Glasgow and London. In 1969 he graduated from the University of Hull, then lived in Germany, before gaining a PhD for 'Myths of Place', a study of landscape in the poetries of Auden and Heaney. He has worked as a writer and editor in business, administration and higher education. He has published three collections of poetry, and his latest, the fourth, *Beyond the Playing Fields* (Shoestring, 2010), is reviewed in this issue.

Tim Liardet has produced seven collections of poetry. *The Blood Choir,* his fifth collection, won an Arts Council England Writer's Award as a collection-in-progress in 2003, was a Poetry Book Society Recommendation for Summer 2006 and shortlisted for the 2006 TS Eliot Prize. His pamphlet, *Priest Skear,* appeared last year and was the Poetry Book Society Pamphlet Choice for Winter 2010; llegory, is due in 2010., s brother who died young and in mysterious circumstancescal *The Storm House* is due from Carcanet in 2011. He is Professor of Poetry at Bath Spa University.

Melinda Lovell lives, gardens, walks and writes in the foothills of the Cantal, South West France. She has had poems published in a variety of magazines and was short-listed for the Frogmore Poetry Prize in 2008 and 2010. She also runs a chapbook enterprise called Inchivala Press with her younger daughter, Hannah. A chapbook of haikus by Melinda entitled *This* is available from www.inchivalapress.com

Maitreyabandhu is 49 and lives and works at the London Buddhist Centre. He has been ordained into the Triratna Buddhist Order for 20 years, and has written two books on Buddhism. Since 2009 he has won the Keats-Shelley Prize, The Basil Bunting Award, the Geoffrey Dearmer Prize and the Ledbury Poetry Festival Competition. His pamphlet *The Bond* (first-stage winner of The Poetry Business Book and Pamphlet Competition) is due out this month.

Andrew McNeillie's recent book of poems was *In Mortal Memory* (2010). His memoir *Once* appeared in 2009. His several other books include the memoir *An Aran Keening* (2001) and the poetry collection *Slower* (2006). *Agenda* Editions has just brought out, at the same time as this issue, a new poetry collection, *Losers Keepers.*

Tim Murdoch had a brief spell in advertising, then studied and taught yoga and practised shiatsu treatment in the US and Canada. His poetry has been published in many magazines and journals including *Acumen, Agenda, Pulsar, Smith's Knoll, South Bank Poetry* and *The Spectator.* He has performed at venues throughout the UK, the US, Holland, Spain, and with Dolores Creel made poetry programmes for Radio Educación in Mexico City.

Jennie Osborne lives in Totnes, enjoys performing at readings around Devon and is active in local poetry groups. Her work has appeared in a number of anthologies and magazines, including *The Rialto* and *The Shop*, and her first collection, *How to be Naked*, was published by Oversteps Books in 2010.

William Oxley was born in Manchester. A poet and philosopher, he has also worked as accountant, part-time gardener, and actor. His poems have been widely published in magazines and journals as diverse as *The New York Times* and *The Formalist* (USA), *The Scotsman, New Statesman, The London Magazine, Stand, The Independent, The*

Spectator and *The Observer*. A former member of the General Council of the Poetry Society, he is consultant editor of *Acumen* magazine and on the organizing committee of the Torbay Poetry Festival. He was Millennium Year Poet-in-Residence for Torbay in Devon. He has co-edited the anthology *Modern Poets of Europe* (Spiny Babbler, Nepal 2004); and in 2004, Hearing Eye published *Namaste* his Nepal poems. A study of his poetry, *The Romantic Imagination*, came out in 2005 from Poetry Salzburg. A fine, limited edition of his *Poems Antibes* was launched in Antibes, Côte d'Azur in December 2006. In 2008 he received the Torbay ArtsBase Award for Literature. His latest collection is *Sunlight in a Champagne Glass* (Rockingham Press, 2009). His work is featured on various websites, including www.creativetorbay.com and www. poetrypf.co.uk

Ian Parks was one of the Poetry Society New Poets in 1996. His collections include *Shell Island, Love Poems 1979-2009*, and *The Landing Stage* (reviewed by David Cooke in the last 'Hoofmarks' issue of *Agenda*, Vol 45 No 3). A new collection, *The Exile's House*, is due from Waterloo Press this year.

Phillip Pass recently obtained his doctorate from the University of St Andrews for a thesis entitled 'The Language of self – Strategies of Subjectivity in the novels of Don DeLillo'. In addition to his work on contemporary American literature, he has also written and presented on a range of topics including Eighteenth and Nineteenth century literature, and British and American ecological writing.

Lynn Roberts is an art historian specializing in the history of picture frames, and is co-author of *A History of European Picture Frames* and *Frameworks* (both 1996). She has essays on frames in the recent catalogue raisonné of Ford Madox Brown by Mary Bennett, and in the catalogue of the exhibition *The Cult of Beauty*, which opened recently at the V & A. She has won the Listowel Writers' Week Poetry Collection competition, the Pulsar Poetry Competition and the Northampton Literature Group Competition, and has just published a sequence of poems, *Rosa Mundi*, and a book of light verse, *Pandora's Book* (InVerse, 2011).

Tony Roberts was educated in England and America. He has published three poetry collections: *Flowers of the Hudson Bay* (Peterloo), *Sitters* (Arc) and, in 2010, *Outsiders* (Shoestring Press). His poems, reviews and essays appear regularly in the literary press.

Robin Robertson is from the north-east coast of Scotland. His fourth collection of poetry, *The Wrecking Light*, was published in 2010 and was shortlisted for the Costa, the Eliot and the Forward Prize. His translation of *Medea* was staged at the Dublin Fringe Festival and dramatised by RTÉ. He has received a number of accolades, including the E.M. Forster Award from the American Academy of Arts and Letters and all three Forward Prizes.

Jaime Robles published her most recent book of poetry, *Anime, Animus, Anima*, with Shearsman Books (2010). Her work has been published in numerous magazines, among them *Conjunctions, Jacket, New American Writing, Shadowtrain* and *Volt!* She has produced many of her texts as artist books, and her bookworks are in many special collections, including the Bancroft Library, Berkeley; The Beinecke Library, Yale University; and the Oulipo Archive in Paris. A native of the San Francisco Bay Area, she is currently living in Exeter.

202

India Russell read German and Scandinavian Studies at University College, London and was appointed Junior Research Fellow in German at King's College, London. She holds a Speech & Drama Licentiate at Guildhall School of Music and Drama and trained in Contemporary Dance at The Place. She toured her own one-woman dance-drama on Ibsen's last plays, using her own translation. Her work is published in many journals and her first collection of poetry, *The Kaleidoscope of Time*, went into its third impression in 2010 when her second collection, *The Dance of Life*, was also published. Her poetry has been translated into Persian for *Kimia*, a book of mystic poetry and prose and she has just completed her third collection, *The Lane to Paradise*. Virginia McKenna has recently recorded some of her work.

Omar Sabbagh is an Arab/British poet. His poetry has appeared in and/or is forthcoming in other quality poetry journals, such as *Poetry Review*, *PN Review*, *The Reader, Stand*, *The Warwick Review*, *Banipal*, *Poetry Wales* and elsewhere. His first collection, *My Only Ever Oedipal Complaint*, was published by Cinnamon Press in September 2010, and his second collection, *The Square Root of Beirut*, is forthcoming with Cinnamon Press in February 2012.

Fiona Sampson's *Rough Music* was shortlisted for the 2010 Forward and T.S. Eliot Prizes. Forthcoming in May are *Percy Bysshe Shelley* (Faber) and *Music Lessons: The Newcastle Poetry Lectures* (Bloodaxe). *Beyond the Lyric,* a critical survey of contemporary British verse, will appear from Chatto in autumn 2012.

James Simpson won second prize in the Thomas Hardy Society's James Gibson Memorial Poetry Competition. He has collaborated with the artist and printmaker Carolyn Trant on an artist's book, *Hunting the Wren* (Parvenu / Actaeon Press). *The Untenanted Room* has just been published by *Agenda* Editions.

Peter Sirr lives in Dublin where he works as a freelance writer and translator. His most recent collection of poems is *The Thing Is*, published by The Gallery Press in 2009, for which he was awarded the Michael Hartnett Prize in 2011. The Gallery Press has also published *Marginal Zones* (1984), *Talk, Talk* (1987), *Ways of Falling* (1991), *The Ledger of Fruitful Exchange* (1995), *Bring Everything* (2000), *Selected Poems* and *Nonetheless* (both 2004). He is a member of Aosdána.

Will Stone is a poet and translator currently residing in Brussels. His first collection of poems *Glaciation* (Salt Publishing) won the international Glen Dimplex Award for poetry in 2008. His second collection *Drawing in Ash* has just been published by Salt. A first English translation of Stefan Zweig's European travel essays, *Journeys* was published by Hesperus Press in October 2010. Two further works of translation, the *Selected Poems* of Belgian symbolist era poets Emile Verhaeren and Georges Rodenbach are about to appear from Arc Publications.

Alan Stubbs was born in Salford, Lancashire in 1962 and he has lived in Cumbria for the last 22 years. His poems have been commended in several major poetry competitions, including the Arvon and Bridport competitions. His poems have been published in *Poetry Review*, *The Rialto*, *Poetry Monthly* as well as in other journals. He also appears in *Into a Gathering*, a collection of poetry from Cumbria.

Warren Stutely (born West London, 1946) lives in Teddington. After studying composition, vocal technique and piano at the Guildhall School of Music, he was a specialist bookseller for 30 years, until, more recently, his knowledge of early English music, art and culture led to his working at Hampton Court Palace. His main interests are English history, especially the early church, and modern/living British composers and painters, particularly the St Ives School.

Siân Thomas lives in East Sussex. Her work has appeared in a number of publications, including *The Daily Telegraph* and *Swamp*, and she holds a Masters degree in Creative Writing and Authorship from the University of Sussex. Among other projects, she is currently working on a collection based upon Ovid's *Metamorphoses* and is a member of Four Quarters, a collaborative arts group that aims to document the cycle of the seasons in a Sussex woodland.

Mark Totterdell works as a copywriter and lives in Devon. His poems are inspired by the landscapes and wildlife of South West England.

Andrew Waterman was born in London in 1940. After a miscellany of clerical and manual jobs, he read English Literature at Leicester University in his mid-twenties, and from 1968 to 1997 taught at the University of Ulster. He now lives in Norwich. Most recent among his nine collections of poetry are his *Collected Poems* and *The Captain's Swallow*, both published by Carcanet Press. He has also written much critical prose. Andrew Waterman is a recipient of the Cholmondeley Award for Poets. His website is at www.andrewwaterman.co.uk

Lynne Wycherley's newest collection *Poppy in a Storm-struck Field* is published by Shoestring Press (ed. John Lucas, Nottingham). She was voted an 'alternative generation poet' (Staple); and her recent prizes include the Second Light Competition (j. Pauline Stainer) and the Fellows' Poetry Prize. She recently featured in *Soul of the Earth* (Awen, 2010, ed. Jay Ramsay).

Samantha Wynne-Rhydderch's second collection, *Not in These Shoes*, was shortlisted for Wales Book of the Year 2009. Her third collection will be published by Picador in Spring 2012.

Look up to catch eclipses, gold leaf, comets,
angels, chandeliers, out of the corner of your eye
from 'Of Mutability', title poem from Jo Shapcott's award-winning collection

WOMEN'S POETRY COMPETITION 2011

1st prize £2,000

plus a week at the idyllic poets' writing retreat of Cove Park
and a mentoring afternoon with the editor of premier poetry
magazine, *Poetry Review*

2nd prize £400, 3rd prize £200

20 other finalists will each receive £25 and all winning
poems will be published in *Mslexia* magazine

Judge: Jo Shapcott

Closing date: 18 July 2011
For entry details visit www.mslexia.co.uk
email poetry@mslexia.co.uk
or call 0191 233 3860

FOR WOMEN ● WHO WRITE

The best place to discover what's happening in contemporary poetry

Poetry Review is the UK's poetry "magazine of record", with poetry, essays and reviews from the best poets and critics from Britain and around the world.

Recent contributors include John Burnside, Mahmoud Darwish, Carol Ann Duffy, Bernardine Evaristo, Seamus Heaney, Don Paterson, Jo Shapcott and Richard Wilbur.

A UK annual subscription to *Poetry Review* (four issues per year) costs as little as £30. Subscribe today and never miss an issue.

To subscribe, telephone 020 7420 9881 or
email membership@poetrysociety.org.uk
www.poetrysociety.org.uk

TEAR–OFF SUBSCRIPTION FORM

Pay by cheque (payable to 'Agenda'), or
Visa / MasterCard

SUBSCRIPTION RATES ON INSIDE FRONT COVER

1 Subscription (1 year) =

| 2 double issues |
| 1 double, 2 single issues |
| or ⁻ |
| 4 single issues |
| (The above is variable) |

Please print

Name: ....

Address: ....

....

....

.... Postcode ....

Tel: ....

Email: ....

Visa / MasterCard No: ☐☐☐☐ – ☐☐☐☐ – ☐☐☐☐ – ☐☐☐☐

Expiry date: ☐☐ – ☐☐

Please tick box:

New Subscription ☐   Renewed Subscription ☐
(or subscribe online – www.agendapoetry.co.uk)

Send to: AGENDA, The Wheelwrights, Fletching Street, Mayfield,
East Sussex, TN20 6TL
Tel: 01435-873703